PRAYING
with
ACCURACY

PRAYING
with
ACCURACY

Ministering to the Needs of Others Through Prayer

RICK A. BONFIM

Rick Bonfim Ministries
P.O. Box 5188
Athens, GA 30604

I dedicate this book to my wife, Mary Lucy Bonfim. She has been faithful and courageous in this journey with me as a full-time evangelist. This book is also dedicated to my children: Rick Jr. and his wife, Laura; Sammy and his wife, Cindy; and Sandy and her husband, Tom. I thank my kids for understanding why Dad was always gone on the weekends.

Contents

Foreword

If prayer is best defined as a conversation or communication between God and human beings, then this book is about placing its readers in a posture to speak honestly with God about the needs of others while allowing the Holy Spirit to choose to respond to prayer as God determines. It is an emptying of one's self of our preconceived ideas and notions about God's answers to our prayers. This can be difficult for those shaped, formed, and educated within traditional Western Christian theology or even just Western education period.

Our starting point is what often hinders us: our deeply rooted worship of scientifically verifiable data. I can see some of you cringing even now, if not physically, at least intellectually. It is Rick's section on rejection not rebellion that I think is critical to praying with accuracy. I ask you to please notice I didn't mention seeing miracles, I said *praying with accuracy*. This book is designed not to teach you to perform miracles, but to help you see prayer as a God-given instrument to meet the needs of those with whom we come in contact each and every day. It is designed to relieve some of the first-year frustration many pastors feel that eventually becomes a lifetime of frustration or even causes burnout or early retirement. It is for laity that need to know that God expects you to use the gift of prayer to minister to the needs of your family members, friends, coworkers, fellow church members, and strangers. It is a book that I highly recommend to ecclesiastical leaders struggling with what we know today as adaptive issues. These are issues that have no predetermined answers. These are issues and people that stretch us beyond our capacity.

In a time like today when doing church as usual is being rejected by so many millennials and younger generations, I truly believe we should pray just as the disciples prayed in the first century when they faced new challenges such as the lame man by the Beautiful Gate: "Peter said, 'I don't have any money, but I will give you what I do have. In the name of Jesus Christ the Nazarene, rise up and walk!'" (Acts 3:6 CEB).

People don't need to see us—they need to see that God gives answers we don't possess.

James E. Swanson Sr.
Resident Bishop
The Mississippi Annual Conference
The United Methodist Church

Preface

For they disciplined us for a short time as seemed best to them, but He disciplines us for our good, so that we may share His holiness.

—Hebrews 12:10

I left Athens, Georgia, in the middle of the night and arrived in Brookhaven, Mississippi, just in time for the evening service. The service was about to begin and the pews were filled with the saints. The pastor welcomed me to the pulpit. The organist started with the opening song and soon it was time for me to speak.

My text came from John 11, the resurrection of Lazarus, and I made an invitation for those who felt they were spiritually detached from God. The response was overwhelming when more than 90 percent of those attending came forward. As they knelt at the chancel rail, I saw so many faces. Before me were faces filled with fear, faces trying to hide anger, faces with sadness, and faces revealing trauma and hurt.

Every person I prayed for that night left an impression upon me. I remember that my inability to connect to the needs of so many was disheartening to me. They had come seeking guidance and direction, and I did not know how to say anything that would truly help them change their lives. So I sat in the chair near the pulpit and wondered how an evangelist should function. I refused to make up prayers that came from my head, all of those eloquent prayers that were filled with words, but did nothing to ease the burden of people longing for healing and deliverance. I had simply had it with that type of empty mind-based prayer.

My most sincere supplication to the Lord as I returned home after three days in Mississippi was, "God, why is it that I cannot accurately comprehend and minister to the deepest cries of Your people?" That night changed my entire perspective about the importance of being able to pray for others during an altar call. It bothered me that I could not address the problems and pain with sufficiency. The Spirit of God had been convicting a whole congregation, and I had felt completely out of the process, like a standby.

I promised the Lord that I would seek the answers. For a period of many years, I fasted several days a month, waiting on God and asking Him for wisdom. I submitted my life to Him completely. I desperately had to have His help to fathom active, powerful, and effective prayer which would really make a difference in the lives of others. How does it work? Yes, I knew how to talk to God about all kinds of things, but I had no real comprehension as to how to pray for others. One thing became clear to me: the impact of my ministry would come through prayer and not preaching. Many people can preach a beautiful message. But once the Word is given, how does the Christian worker or minister apply that Word to the deepest needs of God's children through prayer ministry?

This book, written over a period of twenty years, is an attempt to share the deep things of God, which I have personally learned and experienced in the area of prayer. I do not claim that it is the *only* way to pray for others. I only know that as I was taught by the Word and the Holy Spirit how to pray with accuracy for specific needs, the fruits began to multiply.

After forty-five years of praying for others, I am now trying to put these lessons on paper. My limitations of language and age might interfere, but my heart is grateful for this opportunity of a lifetime to share what I have learned and experienced with you.

People have been asking for and waiting for this book to be completed for many years. By the grace of God, we have finally put all of these words on paper and sent them to the publisher. Now it is in your hands to study, ponder, pray into, and apply. Are you ready to boldly pursue praying with accuracy in order that you might do the ministry of Jesus and bless the lives of many hurting souls?

I ask you to read this book with an open heart. The abundant fruits which God has given me in my many years of ministry as I have implemented these principles of prayer speak for themselves.

"My Father is glorified by this, that you might bear much fruit, and so prove to be My disciples" (John 15:8).

Acknowledgments

To my dear friends:
Rev. John Freeland and Rev. Joseph Tillman Jr., for without them I would never have begun this project. They heard me teach this material and wrote the first manuscript. Their thoughts and ideas are in this book. I could not translate what the Lord has shown me without them. To Andy Miller of Seedbed Publishing for his great encouragement in making sure this second edition will be a blessing to many. He has gone above and beyond to validate me in what God has called me to do. To Holly Jones of Seedbed Publishing for her attention to detail and great care.

To the staff of RBM:
To Betty McKinney for believing this book is important to the kingdom of God. She has put in countless hours over a period of many years in order to summarize, edit, and clarify my thoughts in order to make this book a reality. To Dr. Frank Appel for suggestions and corrections. To Frankie Appel for her encouragement and support. To Johnathan and Tara Dunn for corrections and suggestions. To Rev. Pam Morrison for additions and corrections done with so much love. To Kathy Fallon for her graphic design work and many hours spent formatting this book for publishing.

To the United Methodist Church:

To the thousands of Methodist people who to this date support, pray, and continue to serve this beloved church with distinction and character.

I am deeply, deeply grateful.

Introduction

As we minister to people through prayer, we make a difference only as we target the real need in a person. As a pass in football must be aimed directly at a receiver, effective prayer must be aimed directly at its target. In football, there are many players who could possibly catch the ball, but a perfect pass to the receiver results in a touchdown. Prayer, as in football, should make a touchdown every time you open your mouth to minister in prayer.

In prayer, what you say must find the target, the need—and not just any need, but the nucleus of the problem of the man, woman, or child receiving prayer. This is only possible if you can pray with accuracy. You cannot begin your prayer with what someone tells you, because the person may not even perceive his or her real need. You cannot begin your prayer by asking God to relieve the consequences of the situation, because that kind of prayer will only address the symptoms of the problem. Rather, you must get to the very essence—the core need that is the single most influential factor affecting the life of the individual before you. Getting to the heart of the need will require the leading of the Holy Spirit and the proper use of Scripture.

I have met many pastors and leaders who conduct counseling for hours each day, only to become worn out from hearing about the same trials and complaints over and over again. These leaders are frustrated as they seem to get nowhere in their goals for spiritual formation and maturity in the people they see. Accurate prayer will take you quickly to the place of greatest need so that you will be able to spend less time in counseling!

Can we as mere humans really do this: pray with accuracy, actually penetrating the heart, the very core, of someone for whom we pray? When our Lord met Nathanael, it was at the invitation of Phillip. What Jesus said to Nathanael opens the possibility that our Lord, in a moment's time, received a revelation from God that instantly convinced Nathanael that Jesus was the Christ, the Anointed One: "Jesus saw Nathanael coming to Him, and said of him, 'Behold, an Israelite indeed, in whom is no deceit!' Nathanael said to Him, 'How do You know me?' Jesus answered and said to him, 'Before Phillip called you, when you were under the fig tree, I saw you'" (John 1:47–48).

If a revelation from God about a person can occur during a simple dialogue, then it can also occur during a prayer. What is important here is that accuracy in ministry will bring results and conviction. I must ask you point-blank: How are your prayers going? How many times have you repeated the same prayer over a variety of situations and hoped for something new and different to happen?

The manner in which Jesus Christ spoke to Nathanael in this dialogue opens the door for us to see that God was speaking accurately to Nathanael through our Lord for a much higher purpose. (Both Phillip and Nathanael became lifelong apostles of Jesus after this encounter.) Jesus Christ never prayed or spoke superficially to anyone. Our prayer must also reach beneath the surface to the very essence of someone in order to fulfill its purpose. Our prayer must reach the center of the soul, to the reality and need of the person, to bring healing and wholeness into the life of the one for whom we pray.

You may ask, "How can this happen?" Simply think about the modern world in which we live. These days you take for granted that you can access a wireless signal, which enables you to surf hundreds of sites on the Internet on your phone or computer. You can also, with the help of an antenna in your car, receive XM radio signal anywhere you are in the country. If such wonders are possible in the world of technology, why is it absurd to think that you, a citizen of the kingdom of God, can receive a signal from heaven? If your computer can receive Wi-Fi, why is it not possible for your spirit to receive information from the Spirit of God, who knows all things? Learning to hear spiritual things from the heart of God will enable you to minister to people in a way that is literally life changing for them.

If you really want to pray effectively and see results, there are several areas we will need to explore through this study of prayer:

1) How God sees us: the heart of God as He ministers to the basic needs of people.

2) How God ministers: the methodology of Jesus Christ in His ministry to others.

3) How the soul responds: how to minister to the soul of a human being.

4) How to break through in prayer: the concept of your authority as a believer.

As we follow the Gospels, we will see and hear the heart of God in the ministry of Jesus Christ. When He was engaged in personal ministry, our Lord used certain language, certain spiritual principles, and certain movements, which formed a repetitive methodology of prayer and ministry. You might see this as being a bit presumptuous on my part, but I am going to state it anyway: when you are tuned in to just how our Lord did ministry, it takes about a minute to get to the source of the problem so that you can pray for someone with accuracy.

In other words, you can minister effectively, efficiently, and powerfully to others just as Jesus did.

There is no more powerful, effectual, balanced methodology than the one used by our Lord! Anyone can minister as Christ did if he or she is willing to accept the principles Jesus established in prayer and personal ministry. By the time you move through the Synoptic Gospels comparing miracle with miracle, dialogue with dialogue, and one act of ministry with another act of ministry, you will realize that the greatest secret of the ages is accessible to *every* seeking heart, if received by faith.

1

The Ministry of Prayer

The Christian religion is hopeless without the Holy Ghost. . . .
Confusion and impotence are the inevitable results when the
wisdom and resources of the world are substituted for the
presence and power of the Spirit.

— Samuel Chadwick

Time and time again in Scripture, we see our precious Savior working miracles. He healed the blind, the lame, the deaf, the mute, the leprous, and He even raised the dead. Obviously, He bestowed physical healing upon multitudes, but He was even more interested in the ministry of wholeness, which involves restoration of the whole person. If the prayer that is offered for someone is insufficient, if it is less than what is required, the person receiving prayer will be deprived of a full blessing. Could you be used by God to release healing, wholeness, and renewal upon the life of someone who is bound and afflicted? Could your prayers to God for others become more powerful and accurate?

The purpose of this book is to deal specifically with prayer that addresses the fountainhead—the very core of people's needs. Learning this scriptural practice of accurate prayer is not some form of spiritualized psychotherapy. It is taught and led entirely by the Holy Spirit and it is based completely upon the ministry of Jesus and the Word of God. I did not develop any of this material by reading a book or studying the methodology of a great leader or evangelist. This material comes out of my lifelong study of the ministry of our Lord Jesus Christ. So, if you are feeling the way I felt that night in Mississippi, if you feel your prayers aren't quite getting through, I invite you to take this journey with me. If you simply run out of words when praying for illness, for the suffering, for the forsaken, for the lost, or when praying for a rebellious child, this book can help you!

I recall hearing the prayer of man over a very ill member of his church, "Lord, Your will be done for Brother John." That was not a very powerful prayer in my opinion. If I get sick, I hope someone will approach me with faith, fearlessness, and fortitude, and address the illness as an enemy! To only ask that God's will be done is to sidestep our responsibility to pray boldly, specifically, and accurately, as Jesus did.

In my last year at seminary I was introduced to the Clinical Pastoral Education program. CPE gave an opportunity for each student to be under supervision, learning how to care for those suffering from illnesses. I really wanted to know if a simple prayer spoken over someone who was severely ill could make any difference. One of my professors at Candler School of Theology in Atlanta, Georgia, suggested to me that I should establish a control group in order to arrive at an accurate conclusion in my experiment. So I set up a schedule of daily visits on one specific floor of the hospital, designating 50 percent of the patients to receive prayer in their visit, and 50 percent to receive no prayer. After the day was over, I would make note of all of those patients who received prayer and record their status.

As I visited the patients daily for ten or more minutes, some were in a coma, so I sang and played my guitar (to the amusement of the nurses). With those who could talk, I would listen to them share their thoughts and memories, and I would share stories of my own childhood. I did all of this with all of the patients. However, I was careful to add prayer for healing with my designated control group every time I visited. When it came time for the prayer, I would never close my eyes. I would watch for any reactions I could observe in the patient, such as tears, movement of hands or feet, movement of the head, and especially their eyes looking back at me. At times in my prayer I would refer to the family of the patient, and pray for the family. The responses were different from one person to another, but when their tears began to flow, I could not deny that something significant was happening. At the end of three months, I was truly amazed with my results. I could not ignore it. More than 90 percent of the ones who had received prayer fared better in comparison than those with whom I visited but did not pray! A very strong suggestion about the power and effectiveness of prayer began to be formed in my mind. That CPE experience in my seminary days, all those years ago, was the very beginning of the material of this book and of all that I want to share with you in the following chapters.

The work of wholeness begins when a person is fully convinced of the supremacy of God above all. In Mark 5:25–34, the woman with an issue of blood was made whole. What does this mean? Her physical suffering was ended (she had been sick for twelve years), but so much more was changed in that brief encounter with Jesus. She was a woman who had "endured much at the hands of many physicians, and had spent all that she had and was not helped at all, but rather had grown worse" (Mark 5:26). For her, there was broken trust in authorities who had no power to help her. She had lost her money and, in that culture, had undoubtedly lost social and religious status with others. Labeled unclean, she lived with the weight of feeling ashamed, rejected, and the social pressure to be secretive. After she courageously reached out and touched the hem of His garment (see Mark 5:28), Jesus called her before Himself and addressed her as "daughter" in front of her peers. He did more than heal her physical affliction. He set her free at her deepest level of suffering. Jesus imparted an intimate touch upon her life so that not only her body was healed, but also her distress, her isolation, her rejection by others, and her attitude about herself. In one grand transaction, He gave her validation, acceptance, dignity, and peace. He imparted wholeness to this woman.

In most of the miracles of Jesus, the information about the need did not come from the person wanting healing; it came from the Holy Spirit. Because God is involved in the actual ministry of accurate prayer, all details, all words, and all attempts to help someone through prayer are not to be initiated by us, but are to be led by the Holy Spirit.

> In the same way the Spirit also helps our weakness; for we do not know how to pray as we should, but the Spirit Himself intercedes for us with groaning too deep for words; and He who searches the hearts knows what the mind of the Spirit is, because He intercedes for the saints according to the will of God. (Rom. 8:26–27)

Think about it this way: if God reveals the root of a problem or illness, He must be already contemplating healing and restoration. It is not within the character of the Holy Spirit to reveal intimate knowledge about a problem just to impress you or make you aware of it. Be certain that when God is revealing, He is also healing—in many instances right there in the middle of your prayer!

In John 14:12, Jesus said, "Truly, truly I say to you, he who believes in Me, the works that I do, he will do also; and greater works than these he will do; because I go to the Father." The pressing question is: Do we genuinely believe these words of Jesus?

The most serious problem in our theology of prayer is that we somehow do our own thing, and do not regard the manner in which Jesus prayed and ministered as the *only* example to be followed. I ask you to consider the following questions: How have you learned to minister to people in need? Who has been your example? Have you been taught to minister the way Jesus did? We must identify our allegiance.

Know this: the approach given in this book is not a charismatic approach. It is a biblical approach, tested by years of praying for thousands of people. The methodology for prayer found in this book might be new to some of you. Because it is based entirely on the ministry of Jesus, I am confident that as you study and apply it, you will begin to see results in your prayer ministry that you have never seen before. I suggest that as we begin, you become willing to set aside all of your learned techniques of prayer up to this moment, and allow the Holy Spirit to teach you something new. I beg you to forgive any inability on my part to explain it more clearly, but in no way should my weakness of expression through language diminish this powerful biblical truth!

I traveled to Israel for the first time in November of 2007. When visiting the Sea of Galilee, I was struck by the idea that the miracle of multiplying two fishes and five loaves was an effort by our Lord Jesus to convince the disciples of His divinity. However, Scripture tells us that their hearts were hardened, and they struggled for a long time with the meaning of His miracles. Yes, it was difficult for the disciples, and it is difficult for us too! However, it is essential that we enter into a new level of faith and willingness if we are to see the Holy Spirit work through us in the same way that He worked through Jesus to restore and change crumbling, troubled lives.

Hearing the Voice of God

If we wish to be able to pray for people accurately, the place to begin is by hearing God. But how? The first task is to separate *our own inner voice* from the voice of God. When our minds are already made up about a certain subject, we tend to hear our personal opinion about something and accept it as the only truth. One's own voice is formed from the many experiences we have had throughout our lives. We respond to ourselves based upon our upbringing and training, our past experiences, our present situation, and our expectations for the future. However, we may or may not have a totally accurate perception of reality. Being aware of one's own voice is critical in discernment, because our own preconceived notions can interfere with hearing the voice of God. Your own rationalization should be the last thing you depend upon.

Second, we must be aware of how we are influenced by *suggestive thinking*. Suggestive thinking comes from outside sources. There are many voices telling us many things all the time. We can hear thoughts that may sound good or feel good but do not please God, do not generate power, and do not accomplish His purposes. Suggestive thinking can produce much confusion.

In Israel, to the east of Jericho, lies the Mount of Temptation. From the top of this mountainous area, you can see the Jordan River where Joshua crossed over to the city of Jericho and marched around its walls. It is a place of desolation. The landscape is dry and barren; there is very little water in sight. The place breathes despair, fear, and loneliness. It was to this area that the Holy Spirit led Jesus Christ to be tempted by the devil, and Jesus used three verses of Deuteronomy to defeat him! We, too, can be taken in our minds to the driest and most desolate of places where faith has not visited. The devil suggested many appealing things to Jesus in order to deter Him from His purpose. If you are being bothered by suggestive thinking, it will comfort you to know that Your Savior withstood a constant barrage of suggestions that were contrary to the will of God for forty days and nights, and He can give you the power to overcome them as well in His name.

One guideline is helpful here: when dealing with spiritual problems, never listen to an outside source without also testing it against the Word of God. The Scripture will clear your mind regarding what you are hearing, for God will never contradict His own Word. Always measure what you are hearing by the Word.

The third voice you will hear is the *voice of the Holy Spirit*. This is the sweetest voice you will ever hear in your life. There is nothing to compare with hearing directly from the Holy Spirit. The precision of what is said will fit the moment like nothing else. It is revealing, compelling, and convincing. Once you have heard from the Holy Spirit, you will not want to hear from anyone else. Reading a good book is like drinking warm water from a saucer. Hearing the voice of the Holy Spirit is like drinking cold, fresh water from a country spring that never stops flowing.

F. B. Meyer, in fact, compared the Holy Spirit's voice not to a country spring but to the "Amazon River flowing down to water a single daisy."[1]

The voice of God is heard when His presence is welcomed. As you worship the Lord, as you pray to Him and call upon Him, be absolutely certain that He also wants to talk with you! Scripture says, "My sheep listen to my voice" (John 10:27 NIV). If you experience the presence of God but feel that you cannot hear God speak, your feelings are being elevated above the truth of God's Word. So, make a correction. It is not by feeling! It is by faith that you commune with God. In worship, your mind is renewed and the voice of God begins to break through (see Romans 12:1–2).

For example, as you worship, some of the words in songs and Scripture might catch your attention; heavenly concepts and thoughts may be quickened to your spirit. This is His voice breaking in. We must hear and experience Him, and align ourselves with Him before we can touch the lives of other people. Andrew Murray advised along this line that prior to prayer for others, we "first be quiet and worship God in His glory. Think of what He can do, how He delights in Christ His Son, and of your place in Him—then expect great things."[2]

Hearing the Holy Spirit is like being away from your mother for many years and then hearing her voice once again. The sound of it is unlike any other voice. It is full of reason, gentleness, and precision. The voice of God bringing you into all truth is even better than the voice of your mother. It is also like the voice of your father communicating to you in a quiet manner. Sometimes, your father did not even have to speak to you; a mere look was enough to let you know what he wanted you to do. Likewise, God speaks to us in ways that no one can adequately explain. When we begin to recognize this and know that He is speaking, our faith will grow. All that we lack, the Holy Spirit can supply because the Holy Spirit is Himself, according to Samuel Chadwick, "The Spirit of God, the Spirit of Truth, the Spirit of Witness, the Spirit of Conviction, the Spirit of Power, the Spirit of Promise, the Spirit of Love, the Spirit of Meekness, the Spirit of Sound Mind, the Spirit of Grace, the Spirit of Glory, and the Spirit of Prophecy."[3]

Studying Scripture

Revelation from the Holy Spirit is the key to a good, powerful prayer. However, revelation alone is not all that is required in order to pray with accuracy. Knowledge of Scripture, which reveals the heart of God, will add to your discernment and increase your accuracy regarding people's needs. We will deal with both of these concepts in great depth later in this book. The more you know the Word of God regarding the true condition of human beings, revelation will increase, and your accuracy will be based upon a fundamental understanding of how God views people. Our prayers are frequently a mile away from the point of need. You will be surprised to discover how much knowing Scripture will help your prayer ministry become tuned into God and accurate. When you build your prayer on biblical principles, you are on solid ground for ministering wholeness to the life of a person asking for relief!

Settle this in your mind: you will have to read and study the Word before you can hear God accurately. When Scripture is kept and treasured in your heart, then your hearing will increase. If you are hearing Scripture first and putting suggestion and rationalization last, hearing God will follow.

You can hear your own voice filled with doubt and rationalization; you can try to work with a suggestive idea that has no biblical foundation; or you can get used to hearing the sweet voice of the Holy Spirit. Which voice have you been listening to most in your efforts to pray and minister to the needs of others? Do you hear yourself and others louder than the voice of the Holy Spirit and the Word of God?

Personal Information

As we approach a situation of ministry, we also can gain some helpful information from the person for whom we are praying. Simply put, the individual in need may share some personal thoughts and history. This is normal, and may serve to warm up the person to be receptive to a touch from God. However, bear in mind that input received from people asking for help is often steeped more in their own perceptions than in reality. The perceptions of a wounded, hurting soul may be far from reality. Therefore, relying solely upon the things that they tell you can interfere with the effectiveness of a powerful experience in prayer ministry.

When an individual in pain provides the direction for prayer, this can actually curtail the prayer. The information is only helpful if it validates or confirms what the voice of the Holy Spirit has communicated to you in the first place.

Also, it is a popular prayer trend today to take a person back to the womb or to childhood through mental regression. However, devoid of revelation from the Holy Spirit, this can be a very dangerous practice that in the end will not set the person free. How can someone in torment and distress know exactly where to go to find the root of his or her problems? This process can cause much damage and confusion to those involved and should be approached with caution. Regression is not only dangerous but should not be practiced by anyone except a trained professional.

In some instances, you may already know a great deal about the individual because of your own personal relationship with him or her. This is often the case in church circles. If you are the pastor of a church, you will get to know your people as you meet them every Sunday in church and through church functions. Even then, it is important to not fully accept your own perceptions and to guard against developing a final conclusion. Even as an experienced minister, you must depend upon the voice of the Holy Spirit, coupled with revelation from Scripture, to truly minister to a person at their greatest point of need.

I want to give you an example. I was called to go to a local hospital to pray for a man who suffered a very serious motorcycle accident. The family was in the waiting room and the doctors were operating on the man. I began to pray for God's hand to be upon the medical procedure which was taking place at that very moment, but suddenly a thought was interjected into my mind that I should address drug usage. So I did. I prayed that the man be set completely free from drugs, especially alcohol. Scriptures about forgiveness came to my spirit, so I also prayed that he would forgive his father for the deep hurt he had caused in this man's life. I then prayed for forgiveness to take place in the whole family.

As I ended the prayer, I saw that the family members were all weeping heavily. Everyone was being affected. So I started to pray for each individual gathered in that waiting room. All of the man's brothers and sisters were there, and every single one of them asked for ministry that day. This is a prayer that made a touchdown! It hit the target, the area of greatest need.

I could have prayed only for the injury of the man who had suffered in the accident, but I heard something much deeper. This is what happens when you pray with accuracy. As you continue to read, I want to exhort you to be open so that you, too, will begin to pray this way. However, one must walk before they can run, so have patience. If you are still reading this book, then be encouraged! You can and will get to the point where you, too, will see your prayer ministry become more powerful, precise, and Spirit-led.

Having said all of this, I believe that the Holy Spirit blesses and ministers in all kinds of situations. He is the Lord and He is sovereign. I have seen countless people blessed by a simple prayer uttered with a pure heart and in good faith. However, we are striving to expand our horizons and learn more about prayer that generates much fruit. In this book, I am sharing a manner of prayer that has enriched my faith and my ministry. It is hard to argue with the results that I have seen over many years.

A woman came to me and told me about a physical condition that had gone on for years and was becoming debilitating. It didn't take long before the Holy Spirit revealed to me that the real culprit was the bitterness this woman had harbored for many years. Anger, depression, and anxiety had intensified the effects of her sickness. She was incapable of recognizing her own bitterness because she had lived with it for so long. It was so normal for her that she could not even recognize it as a problem. This woman needed healing from bitterness before any physical healing could possibly happen. It was a revelation from God that the root of bitterness was the true cause of her illness. When the cause is revealed, 50 percent of the miracle has already taken place. If I know what is at the root of the problem, I am already on the way to a blessing.

Discernment of Spirits

In 1 Corinthians 12:10, Paul lists "discernment of spirits" as one of the three gifts of revelation given by the Holy Spirit. (This gift and other gifts of the Spirit will be further discussed in later chapters, but let us deal with it briefly here to help us understand accurate prayer.) Discernment of spirits is a communication tool used by the Holy Spirit. He acts on your spirit to introduce powerful, supernatural information directly into your thoughts, your act of ministry, your prayer for someone, or even your preaching or teaching. Discernment of spirits is a movement of the Holy Spirit communicating the spiritual status of someone receiving prayer right in front of you. Discernment of spirits will reveal to you the condition of the soul in spiritual terms, godly or ungodly, good or bad.

Why is the manifestation of discernment of spirits so necessary? It is critically important because it is primarily a revelation from God that gives you direction for your prayer. One small factor revealed to you can determine the entire trajectory and the outcome of the prayer. This is a biblical fact. All true ministry begins with discernment. Let us look at a biblical example of how discernment worked in the ministry of Jesus Christ.

When Jesus met Nathanael, He discerned his soul and knew that Nathanael was a man in whom there was no guile, no deceit. This first impression of Nathanael was enough for Jesus to engage in personal ministry and to choose him as one of the disciples. Jesus said to him, "I say to you, you shall see heaven open and the angels of God ascending and descending upon the Son of Man" (John 1:51).

Discernment of spirits applies to the moment; it pertains to what you have in front of you at the present time. The Holy Spirit becomes active as you engage in just talking with someone in need. The voice alone can give all sorts of information about who that person is. When Jesus heard the voice of blind Bartimaeus (see Mark 10:46–52), He discerned immediately that Bartimaeus had tremendous faith. Just hearing the voice of someone—how he speaks, whether he mumbles or articulates clearly—will help you discover a great deal about his faith and his soul. The hands and feet of someone will give even more insight. The eyes are the windows of the soul. What you discern in just a few moments will determine the direction of your prayer or act of ministry and how you will implement it.

Discernment of spirits is not something spooky or some kind of ESP (Extra Sensory Perception).[4] Discernment of spirits merely means seeing as the Holy Spirit of God sees, knowing what the Holy Spirit knows, and hearing what the Holy Spirit says. It is real. It is not a far-fetched idea reserved only for special people. If discernment of spirits is a gift of the Holy Spirit, anyone who has the Holy Spirit living within him should be able to hear and to respond to God as He communicates to His saints. The Holy Spirit is the Spirit of Jesus.

As you begin to recognize the manner in which the Holy Spirit speaks, His ways will become second nature to you, and no other method will replace hearing from the Holy Spirit. It is a matter of allowing the voice of the Holy Spirit to bring revelation to your mind. It is knowing that God is willing to communicate the information necessary for you to complete an act of ministry in His name, which will set someone free. Everyone who is saved by grace has this gift available to him or her. Paul speaks of this in 1 Corinthians 2:10–12:

> For to us God revealed them through the Spirit; for the Spirit searches all things, even the depths of God. For who among men knows the thoughts of a man except the spirit of the man which is in him? Even so the thoughts of God no one knows except the Spirit of God. Now we have received, not the spirit of the world, but the Spirit who is from God, that we may know the things freely given to us by God.

Christ Jesus set an example for us as to how to do ministry. As you study the Gospels, you find a methodology of ministry that is repeated over and over by our Lord. Don't you want to follow Him in ministry? Don't you want to do just as He did, and to pray just as He prayed? Believing that God can truly use you to do the same miraculous acts as Jesus did is a struggle, I know. But we must strive to believe that this can become our reality, for this is what He has promised us in His Word.

There are many examples in the Gospels that show us that Jesus knew the needs of people through the gift of discernment, enabling Him to speak directly to their hearts and minister to them accordingly. Matthew 9:4 says, "Jesus knowing their thoughts said, 'Why are you thinking evil in your hearts?'" Here we see that the Holy Spirit revealed the minds and hearts of the scribes to Jesus through discernment (see also Matthew 12:25; Mark 2:8; Luke 9:47; John 5:42). Discernment is not a mind-reading trick but a gift of the Holy Spirit found continually in the ministry of Jesus. It is also for us!

Following are three valuable principles that may help you understand how the flow of information comes directly to you from the Holy Spirit at the moment of prayer.

Greater Intimacy Improves Hearing

Even within the Christian community there are those who become nervous when we begin to speak of the Holy Spirit. Perhaps they have had some sort of erroneous teaching regarding the person and work of the Holy Spirit. Maybe someone in their lives portrayed a negative interpretation of the Holy Spirit, which turned them off to the subject.

However, as you read this book, I want you to have only positive thoughts as to what God can do for you and through you when you deeply surrender to Him. Remember the words of our Lord Jesus in Acts 1:8: "But ye shall receive power, after that the Holy Ghost is come upon you: and ye shall be witnesses unto me both in Jerusalem, and in all Judea, and in Samaria, and unto the uttermost part of the earth" (KJV).

I deliberately used the King James Version for this verse. Reading other translations, you may have understood the verse to mean that the Holy Spirit will make you a good witness to people, even those living in the uttermost parts of the earth. And indeed, we pray that He will do so! However, notice the text first says, "witnesses unto me." The primary work of the Holy Spirit is to give you personal revelation of *who* Jesus Christ is. The Spirit witnesses to your spirit so that you see and know the Lord Jesus Christ more clearly and intimately. Knowing Jesus Christ better, more accurately and more fully, will automatically increase your ability to hear from His Spirit. The result will be a great deepening of your prayer life and your ability to receive insight from the Spirit when you meet people in need.

The Holy Spirit has a purpose, which is to save and to serve. Intimacy with God and empowerment in your life and ministry begin to grow when you fully accept the person and the work of the Holy Spirit. Discernment increases when you are not obstructing what God wants to do. Discernment increases when you, even not understanding it all, open the door of your heart in this area of prayer. This is done by faith, and by trusting in the promises of God's Word.

R. A. Torrey correctly described the importance of intimacy and being in the presence of God:

> If, then, we would pray aright, the first thing we should do is to see to it that we really get an audience with God, that we really get into His very presence. Before a word of petition is offered, we should have the definite and vivid consciousness that we are talking to God, and should believe that He is listening to our petition and is going to grant the thing that we ask of Him.[5]

God is the giver of gifts.

In other words, God has the patent on all of the activities of the Holy Spirit. You cannot use anything without His permission—because God alone activates the gifts of the Holy Spirit. First Corinthians 12:11 says, "But one and the same Spirit works all these things, distributing to each one individually just as He wills." Thus, the power that operates any spiritual gift depends on God, the Holy Spirit, who alone activates it as He wills.

Think of the last time you updated your cell phone. You had to have the company activate the phone before you could use it, right? If the phone company did not activate the phone on their end, you would have no service. To grasp this is very important, because no one can say that he or she permanently has a gift. The Holy Spirit activates the gifts to flow in us as the needs of others present themselves. If the Holy Spirit causes discernment of spirits to move through us, it is in order that we can be used by Him to help others. The work of the Holy Spirit is always to save and serve those who long for a touch from Him.

The greatest discovery of my life has been that a simple, straightforward expression of my faith can move the heart of God. There was a time that I thought only the great and mighty could be used of God in such powerful ways, but I have discovered that God honors the small and humble servant who is hungry to do His work.

Allow God to be God.

When I use a tool to do a job around the house, it is clear to me that I am not the tool. I am the one who holds the tool in my hands to complete the job before me. Likewise, I am not God. I am only a tool in the hands of God. He is the One with the mind, the skill, and the power that flows through me. I am a servant who allows the Holy Spirit to work through me as He desires to do. Ultimately, this is His work.

Sometimes pride may cause us to take credit for that which He alone deserves the glory. Keep in mind that you are one of His workers, only a tool in His hands. Give God all the credit for the miracles that He brings forth. Do not run from the awesome power of God. Do not let fear or ignorance quench the very power that raised Jesus from the dead (see Ephesians 1:20). Let God be God, and simply enjoy the amazing, marvelous truth that He desires for you to partner with Him in His redemptive work. This is not only humbling, but wonderful beyond words.

William Law, a contemporary of John Wesley, warned that in this age the Holy Spirit would be as rejected by many as Jesus was in His age.[6] We don't want to be among those who resist and miss the Spirit. In the words of Andrew Murray, "Being filled with the Spirit is simply this—the whole personality is yielded to His power. When the whole soul is yielded to the Holy Spirit, God Himself will fill it."[7]

2

The Heart of God Regarding Need

In the first chapter, we emphasized dealing with the basic need in a person. When you pray for someone, your objective is to pray with accuracy concerning what has caused the hurt or the pain. Discernment of spirits, this marvelous gift of the Holy Spirit, opens a communicative channel between you and the Master of the universe, thus God is very much involved in the interaction. God is the One receiving the prayer and the One you are trying to reach. That is the essence of prayer. The prayer is not directed to the person. The prayer is not a psychological exercise of your mind. The prayer is directed to the living God! Prayer is two-way communication with the Lord. If God is the One you are addressing, then His opinion, His ways, and His thinking about the situation are what matters. Your Heavenly Father is the One who should tell you what is going on, and He is the One who will solve the problem for you. Therefore, understanding the heart of God in matters of human need will help you to be in His perfect will—and therefore effective—as you pray.

In the early years of my ministry, I found myself struggling to even begin a prayer for someone. I lost much time in a superfluous use of words that had little or no meaning. I would ramble on, hoping that I would eventually stumble on to something substantial so that I could make my petition to the Lord about the person and his or her problem. I used lofty phrases, interspersed with religious terminology, which was just me desperately trying to say, "God, would you help me here? I am lost trying to be a nice pastor, but in reality I have no clue as to what the real issue is in this person!" When I ran out of things to say and ended up feeling empty and void in the predicament, I would finally say, "Lord, please just bless them," and many times He did. However, in the depths of my heart, I knew I should be able to minister more powerfully.

But as time went on, a very important thought began to make its way into my mind. I began to question whether it all was as complicated as I was making it. Having a bachelor's degree in psychology probably filled my head with all kinds of ideas about the elusive and complex problems in the psyche of a human being. But I began to wonder, since God created all of us in His image with specific purpose, perhaps there is a master blueprint for all mankind. This would mean that, regardless of race, gender, age, or culture, human beings generally experience the same problems. Could there be an inherent pattern of need that is common to man, and could that pattern be discovered? It was here that a miraculous breakthrough began to take place in my life and ministry.

I will never forget a small church in Houma, Louisiana. It was a Sunday night service, and there were four men at the altar. All I could see was the tops of their heads, since they were looking down at the floor. As I began to walk behind the altar rail, I noticed one of them squeezing his hands so tightly that his knuckles were white. That got my attention. I positioned myself in front of the four men and began to pray. Somehow I knew that these men had a specific issue in common, and I wanted to know what it was. In my heart I heard these words, "Their problem is spiritual." It was like a light bulb came on in my head. I had just had a revelation from heaven!

Still, I didn't know how to deal with it. My mind was racing and my thoughts were going in every direction. Then, a few moments later, a Scripture came to my mind: "And you shall love the Lord your God with all your heart, and with all your soul, and with all your mind, and with all your strength" (Mark 12:30). What this told me in an instant was that these men all had a love for something else above God, which offended the Holy Spirit. I immediately asked the four men a question: "What in your life is offending the Holy Spirit? It is critical to your peace." One of them looked at me and said, "Rick, all of our wives have died during this past year, and we cannot get out of the cemetery. We go there every day." I knew that God detests communication with the dead. It is forbidden in Scripture. The men were still mourning, which was completely normal, but there was something strange about their relationships with their late wives. They were actually trying to maintain communication with their wives by going to the cemetery daily. That was very offensive to the Holy Spirit! These men had a spiritual problem!

This experience was a tremendous and exciting moment of revelation in my prayer ministry. I knew that God had been speaking to me, and yet, until this time I had not gotten the message. Now it flashed before me. Through one passage of Scripture, Jesus had diagnosed the core of all human need.

Let us look at that powerful Scripture in its entirety:

One of the scribes came and heard them arguing, and recognizing that He had answered them well, asked Him, "What commandment is the foremost of all?" Jesus answered, "The foremost is, 'Hear, O Israel! The Lord our God is one Lord;

and you shall love the Lord your God with all your heart, and with all your soul, and with all your mind, and with all your strength.' The second is this, 'You shall love your neighbor as yourself.' There is no other commandment greater than these.'" (Mark 12:28–31)

In the parallel passage of Matthew 22:40, Jesus adds, "On these two commandments depend the whole Law and the Prophets." Now, a glorious insight came to me from the Holy Spirit. What Jesus said to the scribe would solve my quest for clarity in prayer. If we receive this Scripture at face value, it reveals that all human need is fundamentally divided into two areas: some of us have a problem with God, and some of us have a problem with others! When Jesus said, "There is no other commandment greater than these" (Mark 12:31), He was not only summarizing the Law but indicating that the entire Law and everything given through His prophets point to these two great commandments. To be able to observe these two commandments fulfills the purpose of our heavenly Father for mankind, who are made in His image. This is wholeness. To the degree one cannot fully love God (and receive His love) and love others (and receive love), he or she is broken, impaired, and in need.

To put it another way, every person will be able to fulfill and please the heart of God if he can do two things: love God and love his neighbor. John Wesley described the person completely fulfilling these two commandments as the "altogether Christian."[1]

That breakthrough with those men that evening in Louisiana was phenomenal for me. From that day forward, I had a place to begin in prayer. I would no longer search the depths of my mind trying to figure out someone's problem and then begin looking for words to say in prayer. I would no longer have to interview the person to get all of the details (often distorted by perception or deception) about his or her life. The discernment of spirits would point me directly toward the area within the person that cried out for prayer. The Holy Spirit could communicate with me, since I now understood biblically how He views people and their needs. That was enough to begin a whole new life of praying with accuracy. I had some direction!

Though life may bring us different experiences, trials, and difficulties, at the core, Scripture shows us that the heart of a human being is made whole and complete in these two areas: relationship with God and relationship with others. Putting it into even more plain language, all human problems are divided into two categories: spiritual or relational. We suffer because sin separates us from God, and sin hurts our relationships with other people. In one succinct sentence: Your problem is with God or your problem is with others. Prayer with accuracy starts there. It started there for me.

To make sure that I was on the right path, I spent months in careful examination of the law of Moses given in the books of Exodus, Leviticus, Numbers, and Deuteronomy. I discovered that every single law and ordinance in that complex system falls into one of two categories: (1) relating to God in obedience, reverence, and holiness or (2) relating to other people in the manner prescribed by God.

This had an enormous impact on my life. For years my sermons had been fine. The problem that frustrated me was what I should do when people came needing prayer. I so wanted to begin to pray with more accuracy, not grasping and guessing, but effectively ministering to the real needs of real people. When this simple but profound revelation of the Law came, discernment of spirits began to *move* in my prayers! Scripture works alongside Holy Spirit revelation. The Word produces more revelation, and revelation enlightens the Word. When I decided to put my faith exclusively in what God reveals from His Word and what He reveals through the Spirit, hearing from God increased exponentially. Gradually, I began to *expect* specific, accurate revelation from the Holy Spirit every time I opened my mouth to pray for someone.

Once I prayed with a young lady in Curitiba, Brazil, and a revelation came to me that she had experienced deep rejection from others, most likely her husband. I asked the Lord to intervene in her family, especially with her husband, and her tears began to flow. Again I heard the word *spiritual*. At this I paused. How could being rejected by family or a husband be a spiritual problem? I asked her how long it had been since she had come to church. She said that this was the first time in many months. As I drove to the hotel that night, a thought came to me: *Could her separation from God be related to the rejection from her husband?* The answer came just as quickly: "Yes, her rejection of God was directly related to the rejection she had suffered from her husband." She was having difficulty relating to God because she felt so rejected as a person. The rejection she had experienced at the hand of man had caused her to disbelieve God's love for her. Now my mind was opened to a new way to pray. The source of rejection may have been her husband, but her real problem was with God. She had separated herself from Him. The spiritual problem had to be addressed if she was to receive healing.

Seeing People as God Sees Them

Jesus knew the heart of every person He met, and He also knew that the key to healing of all personal suffering was identified within Scripture. If we want to minister to the needs of human beings the way Jesus did, we must see them as God sees them, which is biblically. Jesus was the perfect fulfillment of the Law—the only one able to fully love God and to love others with perfect love. Jesus came to earth and went to the cross in order to restore us in those areas where sin has brought pain and destruction to our lives. Romans 3:20b tells us, "through the Law comes the knowledge of sin." The Law is not able to bring healing to us. We can never be made whole by trying to keep the Law! Scripture is clear on that point. However, the Law pinpoints our greatest area of need—and that need is either spiritual or relational.

What I had been asking from the Lord was how I could minister to His people based upon biblical, revealed truth and not on human education, philosophy, or perception. How could God possibly be wrong in defining human need? I simply decided that I would continue to learn how to pray for people the same way Jesus did, addressing the core issue. When your prayer addresses a problem that has been clearly identified by Scripture, you are on safe ground. God cannot be wrong about this!

Think of it this way: if you own a Mercedes and it develops serious problems with the engine, where would you take it to be serviced? Would it make sense to take it to the Ford dealership? No offense to Ford here, but it seems to me that it would be best to take your car to a Mercedes dealership, because they would understand the car better than anyone else. To pray with accuracy for human beings, you must go the Maker of human beings. The Maker can show you in an instant what is really wrong with an individual. No one knows all about you and your plight better than God! As the Lord examines a human being, He knows exactly what is wrong and how we have broken our relationships with Him and with others. God is the best one to fix humans. God also can communicate with you how to proceed in prayer for someone else so that your service is effective and accurate.

Effectual prayer for any individual must begin with the need, either spiritual or relational. General as it may seem, if you identify which one of these two applies to someone, you will be able to begin to pray for him or her with power. In order to minister to someone and have lasting results, you must relate to the condition in its most primal form. This means discerning whether it is spiritual (with God) or relational (with others). Not only is the Holy Spirit with you in this but also the Word. The Holy Spirit works through the Word and He responds to the Word. Scripture reveals the heart of God toward the human condition and confirms to you what you hear from the Holy Spirit. There are many examples in Scripture that help us grasp both spiritual need and relational need. Let us take a closer look.

Spiritual Need

In all of the histories and cultures of humanity, you will find a variety of gods. People will try anything to reach their Creator. For centuries, man has tried to find and identify the one who created him and to comprehend His ways. This is the greatest human quest: to find God. Perhaps you are one who is on this quest right now. Your deepest desire is to relate to and communicate with God the Creator, to worship Him, and to experience His glory in unbroken fellowship with Him. When we cannot or will not relate to God as we were meant to, a spiritual need is formed.

The story of Saul classically illustrates a spiritual need. God said to Samuel, "About this time tomorrow I will send you a man from the land of Benjamin, and you shall anoint him to be prince over My people Israel" (1 Sam. 9:16). Saul was a man of the highest qualifications. He was a Benjamite, the son of Kish, and the grandson of Abiel. He was an impressive young man without equal among the Israelites, standing a head taller than any of the others (see 1 Samuel 9:2). Saul seemed to do well until his faith in God was tested. Since God chose Saul and sent him to Samuel, we might assume that Saul knew God and possessed a relationship with Him. What we come to learn is that so much fear resided in Saul's heart, the fear overshadowed his faith. What qualifies a servant is the heart. If you follow Saul's story to the end (see 1 Samuel 28), you will discover that he moved so far away from God that he ended up with a compulsion to conjure up the spirit of the deceased Samuel through the Witch of Endor. This was a bad ending for someone who should have, by all human standards, been a tremendous success.

As we get to know Saul, it doesn't take us long to see that he had a serious crisis in his life, which was his lack of intimacy and relationship with the Lord. Saul did not trust in and depend upon the living God. He did not receive his identity from God. Consequently, Saul lived a life full of insecurity, paranoia, and rebellion, lost God's favor, and died in the process. Saul's most dangerous problem was not the Philistines, the enemy that threatened Israel, but rather his constant propensity to disobey God. He had a very deep and serious spiritual need: a broken relationship with God.

You could say that Saul rejected God and, therefore, he became rebellious toward Him. When Samuel instructed Saul to wait for his return before he offered the burnt offering (see 1 Samuel 13:8–11), Saul did not wait for fear of the Philistines. Even though he was a mighty and anointed warrior and king, Saul trembled at the sight of his enemies. He may have been tall and handsome, but inside, he was insecure and afraid. We must recognize what was deep under the surface: Saul felt rejection of self in his life.

Rejection of self and rejection of God are interrelated. It begins with rejection of self. When you cannot accept who you are due to personal or family problems, the response can be to turn against God and to blame Him for your inability to deal with life. The deceptive idea that God is rejecting you and that He is hurtful (like family members may have been) can take root in your soul. So out of that anger and pain, you in turn begin to reject the One who loves you most.

This man Saul was called of God to be the king of Israel. However, he had a spiritual problem. How would you pray for Saul? If you had this privilege, where would you begin in order to reach his heart? There is some information in the biblical account about his upbringing, and that can be helpful. He was the son of Kish, the grandson of Abiel, the great-grandson of Zeror, and of the tribe of Benjamin. This information can tell you a lot. Evidently Saul came from a godly lineage. However, when we meet him in 1 Samuel 9:1–3, he was given the task of the lowest servant: to go looking for some lost donkeys. Could it be that Saul felt diminished and unappreciated by his own father? However it came about, the core of the matter is that Saul's problem was of a spiritual nature. This becomes clear as his story unfolds. Here is where your prayer with accuracy begins, as you invite the Holy Spirit to invade your mind with the very words you are to speak in prayer, bringing forth a wonderful exchange of glory. Prayer is powerful if it reaches its goal. Yes, Saul may have had a problem with his father, with David, and with his enemies. But ultimately his conflict was not with his peers, but with God.

If you find a Saul in the world today, perhaps in your church, this could be a way to begin to pray:

Father, in the name of Jesus Christ Your Son, I reprimand all rejection of Your love, which causes my brother to question You all the time. I stand against all fear, unbelief, and nervousness. Still the heart of this man to know who You truly are and to accept Your love. Remove from his heart the desire to do his own will. I stand against all doubt, all wavering, and all rationalization.

Restore a desire in his heart to please You, O God! Bring a spirit of surrender to Your will. I release faith, which comes by revelation of who You are, into his life. In the strong name of the one who dared to die for us all. Amen.

A prayer like this could change history because you actually prayed for what was at the heart of the matter, and it was true. How did you do this? You discovered that the problem was of a spiritual nature, and your ministry of prayer flowed from there. If your Saul receives your prayer, you will have a spiritual touchdown!

We are inundated with spiritual need these days. Many Christians have compromised their faith because they cannot satisfy their hunger for intimacy with the Lord. Feeling rejected and confused, they yearn for a moment of breakthrough with God. Perhaps they have been in church all their lives, but repetitive prayers, which yield no results, and formal words, memorized over years of church services, can leave them feeling empty and unchanged. Many have actually been damaged by morbid theology and irrelevant exercises in religion. A human spirit must experience the presence and movement of the Holy Spirit in order to be satisfied and made whole.

Remember that someone who has experienced rejection may in turn reject God. They may appear to love Him, and try to serve and obey Him, but they are hindered. They are unable to come to Him in simple faith and childlike trust. They are unable to honestly and wholeheartedly accept Him for who He is. They live life like a spiritual orphan. Author Leif Hetland wrote:

> A true orphan knows what it means to live life without the security, stability, and warmth of a physical home. A spiritual orphan is not any different. He is also well acquainted with the feelings of fear, rejection, anxiety, and homelessness even if he has a place to go home at night. This is because the spiritual orphan has come face to face with the real meaning of homelessness—living life without a father.[2]

This void can be addressed as you learn how to pray for someone with a spiritual problem.

When the basic problem is revealed as spiritual, pay attention to how the spiritual need is being expressed. What are some of the indications of a spiritual need? The person may ask questions about the nature

of God constantly. It seems that the individual analyzes and rationalizes the ways of God every step of the way. He criticizes anything that
requires him to demonstrate faith beyond himself. Anguish comes
when he cannot seem to trust and believe as others do. Therefore,
his mind searches to find answers that will suffice for a moment, but
questions and doubts persist for years. There are those with a spiritual
need who cannot ever conceive of humbling themselves on their knees
as a means of breaking through. They would defend and die for their
theology, even though their beliefs have yielded no lasting fruit in their
lives. When a man or woman of intellect questions elementary matters
of faith, when a mind filled with doubt rationalizes every new biblical
concept, when pride and ego interfere with life, it is very difficult to
accept the simplicity of relationship with God by faith. Some of us
would prefer to relate to a book or a theologian than to God Himself.

For these individuals, your focus in prayer will be upon the
mind, speaking humility, obedience, trust, and healing of the anxious
thoughts. You yourself must approach these souls with peace in your
heart, for peace is something they have never had. A spiritual problem
leaves one who is searching for God confused, frustrated, hopeless, and
ultimately defeated. Make sure you address them with words that will
comfort and encourage. Never pray anyone down; pray them up!

Relational Need

Since Jesus Christ Himself continually dealt with basic needs in
people, it befits us to apply the same method He did. After all, is He
not the Creator and the expert when it comes to His own creation?
Why should we question the fundamental concept of loving God and
loving our neighbor given in Mark 12:28–31 when the Son of God
Himself stated that these two commandments uphold all others? The
secret of a powerful prayer is to begin at the starting point of weakness

and hurt, and without a doubt, these two areas, designated *spiritual* and *relational*, are biblically revealed to be the two areas of greatest need in human beings.

Having dealt briefly with a spiritual need, how then do we identify and minister to a relational need? When Jesus said, "You shall love your neighbor as yourself," He indicated that approximately 50 percent of the underlying problems in human beings are relational. This is intriguing, as 50 percent of the Old Testament commandments involve a problem with father, mother, brother, friend, or others. We are born to live and die within community. None of us has been born to live isolated from others. You are a result of community and you are a part of community; without others your life is not fulfilled.

The relational involves all sorts of human interaction. It includes emotions such as anger, guilt, and hate. It ranges from extended grief to strife, jealousy, envy, and unforgiveness. However, as you begin to pray for a relational need, you will not deal primarily with these emotions, at least not at first. Rather, you will target the relational area that first opened the door to the problem in someone's life. Remember that the Holy Spirit has revealed to you whether the core problem is spiritual or relational; therefore, the Holy Spirit is at work along with you here. Be assured that the Holy Spirit is going ahead of you. He knows precisely where to go. When you address the key area in your prayer, it brings comfort, and the person who is receiving the prayer usually will be open to it. You are the voice, and the Holy Spirit is the one who is convicting the person to accept your prayer.

Let's do a case study from Scripture of someone with a relational need. One example is found in the story of Jacob and his brother, Esau. After stealing his brother's birthright from their father (see Genesis 27), Jacob ran to the house of Laban, far away in Haran. Esau, knowing of the deception of Jacob in order to steal the blessing, held resentment toward Jacob: "So Esau bore a grudge against Jacob because of the blessing with which his father had blessed him; and Esau said to himself, 'The days of mourning for my father are near; then I will kill my brother Jacob'" (Gen. 27:41). This broken relationship between brothers became a matter of hatred and division that lasted for many years. In your dealings with people, you will find those who have received the same treatment as Esau, and they also will not forgive and will not forget.

Jacob worked for Laban for fourteen years to gain his two wives, Leah and Rachel. Jacob was forced to marry Leah first, even though his desire was to marry Rachel. Yet God blessed the union with Leah. She bore Jacob four sons, including Levi, the ancestor of the Aaronic priestly line, and Judah, who produced David's royal line, which includes Jesus Christ. Even though he fulfilled a great destiny, Jacob still carried within him much torment and fear of Esau.

When praying for people with relational problems you might want to use words that will help the person for whom you are praying to better receive your prayer. For example, unforgiveness is associated with anger, distrust, quarrel, strife, revenge, criticism, hardness, and injustice. Those with a relational problem do not have peace in their souls, for there is much that has not been dealt with in the subconscious mind. Your prayer can set the person free from the torture of unresolved relational problems and start them on the way to making things right.

If you encountered Jacob and had the opportunity to pray for him, what would you say? Here is a prayer for your Jacob, who in spite of getting on fairly well with life, still has a deep-seated relational need which must be healed:

Heavenly Father, still Jacob's heart from running from Esau. Give him faith and courage so that he will not be afraid of

Esau, but instead will come to him and ask for forgiveness. Open his mind to understand that staying away from his family will not help anyone; rather, strengthen him to repent of what he has done to Esau. Quiet the waters in this drama and soften the heart of Esau to forgive his brother. Remove all bitterness, hatred, poison, acridity, and strife of any kind from the heart of Jacob, and sustain him to confront his brother in truth and love.

The heart of a prayer for a relational need must address the person who historically was at the center of the relational problem. Over the course of life, we have many relationships; however, one key relationship produces the unrest found in an individual with a relational need. The induction of the problem begins with one person. It could be a mother or father, a grandmother or grandfather, or perhaps a sibling, as in the case of Jacob and Esau. It could be a childhood friend or teacher. As you pray for someone, identify the one individual who caused the most harm and target your prayer toward that person as the key to the inception of a relational need. In the previous biblical case, when healing finally came between Jacob and Esau (Genesis 33), the name of Jacob's mother, Rebekah, did not surface, even though she had been part of the plot against Esau. Jacob had been in full agreement with his mother's plan to deceive his brother. Ultimately, the decision to wrong his brother was made by Jacob himself. Therefore, the healing of this relational problem had to come between Jacob and Esau.

Relational issues can be very damaging to human beings, and the heart of God reveals this when He commands us to "love your neighbor as yourself" (Mark 12:31). You see, man was created to have relationship, and by nature, a man or woman cannot be fulfilled and whole outside of community. We suffer because sin—our sin and their sin— hurts our relationships with people. When your prayer goes directly to this key area of the relational, and addresses it according to biblical truth, it becomes accurate and to the point, and results in changed lives.

You are learning the mind of the Holy Spirit, and from the moment you begin to pray with basic needs in mind, you will not wander off to other places in your prayer ministry. We have used the analogy of a touchdown in football. Getting to the need is similar to a running back reaching the end zone. There is a sense of urgency! You must hurry with it in order to proclaim the critical word in prayer that will convict the individual that the Holy Spirit knows him or her intimately. This is a comforting and exhilarating moment in someone's spirituality, for it is God coming down to that person in the midst of a prayer. You see, when the Holy Spirit reveals, He also heals. When He heals, He also convicts the person receiving the prayer. Your prayer is not a human, fleshly work. It is not something you conjure up out of your mind, will, and emotions. It is a conduit that carries truth directly from the holy and loving heart of God into the deepest corner within a human being. If your computer can receive the power and access of a Wi-Fi signal right now, why can't your spirit access the powerful signal from God which will make you a blessing in the life of someone else? It can. Only believe!

3

The Four Roots

In the previous chapter, we looked at basic needs, which are divided into two major areas: spiritual needs, which pertain to God, and relational needs, which pertain to others. When dealing with the spiritual, you are faced with the biblical mandate to "Love the Lord your God with all your heart, and with all your soul, and with all your mind, and with all your strength" (Mark 12:30). Human beings are created to love their Father, and yet we struggle to do so because of our fleshly nature, the influence of evil, and what life has done to us. If mankind has a problem, it is loving God with all of our being. You must simply name the basic need here, which is that man is rebellious toward God. Prayer regarding this area is a defining moment in the life of the one who is longing for wholeness, for it deals with the very heart of our God. He wants you to be defined by Him. Identity and wholeness can only be found in Him.

A spiritual need is divided into two areas: rejection of self and rejection of God (which is rebellion toward God). Any attitude toward God in turn reflects an underlying attitude toward self. When you can identify either the root of rejection of self or the rejection of God as a basic need, it will open the way and guide your prayer toward deeper places within the heart of the person.

Rejecting God begins with rejecting oneself. When someone is rejected as a person, he or she is prone to reject God. How one relates to God develops out of how one perceives oneself. It is impossible to relate in love to God with all of your heart, all of your soul, all of your mind, and all of your strength when you cannot relate to yourself. The rejection of God is a basic need, which is formed when a person cannot maintain a relationship with God due to personal inner conflict. A person who rejects God is essentially in rebellion against Him.

Relational issues involve your relationship with other people. Jesus emphasized this area when He quoted the law saying, "The second is this, 'You shall love your neighbor as yourself.' There is no other commandment greater than these'" (Mark 12:31). We are communal beings, and outside of community we find ourselves incomplete and unfulfilled. Every one of us has experienced conflict with others or troubled relationships within family. Of course, the degree of the trauma in relation to others varies. However, when the trauma overwhelms or defines a person, a relational need can be created.

If Cain could have resolved his problem with Abel when God gave him opportunity, the first homicide in the Bible would not have occurred. If Esau could have spent time with Jacob and worked out their differences, we could have skipped a sad chapter in human history, which divides nations and incites violence even today. The issues of unforgiveness and the painful consequences are found time and time again throughout Scripture.

There are two areas, or branches, within a relational need: unforgiveness and bitterness. Unforgiveness becomes progressive in its development, establishing an increasingly negative and destructive hold upon the human soul. Unforgiveness can evolve into hatred and bitterness. Because bitterness is unforgiveness that has been allowed to remain and become deeply entrenched, even throughout generations, we can say that unforgiveness is the seat of bitterness. Keep this in mind.

These are the four underlying roots of human need: rejection of self, rejection of God, unforgiveness, and bitterness. If you are thinking this way as you approach a person, with discernment of spirits operating, the Holy Spirit will lead you toward one of these four roots. *What is a root?* A root is the primary area of need where your prayer for wholeness should be directed. Rejection of self and rejection of God could be visualized as vertical roots because they primarily affect our relationship with God. Unforgiveness and bitterness would then be horizontal roots because they directly affect our relationships with others. When praying for a person, you must trust in the manifestation of discernment of spirits to hear what the immediate need is (spiritual or relational).

Let me pause here to address a question that may have just come up in your mind: *How can I be sure that I will hear anything from the Lord?* In other words, What assurance can we possibly have that the Holy Spirit will move to help us understand the most crucial needs of others? The answer is this: the Word has already told us that the basic need of every man and every woman is to love God and to love others. The Holy Spirit will always confirm the Word. Always! If you have the Word foremost in your mind as you step out in faith to pray for another individual, God through the Holy Spirit will honor, enlighten, and verify His own Word every time!

So, after discerning whether the need is spiritual or relational, the next move is to target the root of the problem: rejection of self, rejection of God, unforgiveness, or bitterness. That root is the area where the Holy Spirit will now concentrate and begin to work, giving you whatever information you need to formulate an accurate prayer, which will deeply touch and pierce the very soul of the individual.

Many years ago when visiting Brazil on a mission trip, we were holding a service at a local Methodist church. The sanctuary was filled to the brim, and the team prayed for everyone who came to the altar. The lines of those wanting prayer stretched down the aisles, and our group ministered for almost four hours to make sure that every person would receive prayer, with no one overlooked. The evening was finally over and we were in our bus, very tired and ready to go home to the mission base and to our beds. I was just getting settled in my seat for the long drive home when I noticed a woman knocking on the door of the bus. She was calling out that she wanted me to pray for her! I was tired, and I have to honestly tell you that it did not please me to have to get up and pray for someone when we had already prayed for so long and given every opportunity for anyone in distress to receive attention. However, I did get up and when I came to the door, she said, "Lord, show this man my problem." To tell the truth, I really felt like returning to my seat and closing the door, but the inner voice of God spoke tenderly and kindly to me about her need: it had to do with others. I was immediately convicted. I knew that a revelation had come to me.

Now I had to know how to proceed in my prayer for her. I asked her to look straight at me, and her face showed the scars of many years of pain. I knew that she hated someone with a vengeance, and that her heart was broken. I asked her to answer one question for me, "Tell me his name." Her face distorted with anger and tears began to flow. She exploded in a barrage of words about Antonio, who had left her with four children. I knew she was filled with unforgiveness and much bitterness toward Antonio. Our group came out to pray for her, and the glory of God came upon this woman as she forgave her ex-husband. Then a young man came over and thanked me for bringing healing to his mother. It was the first time she had ever come to a worship service. She not only received Jesus Christ as her Savior that night, but found herself reconciled to a loving God who could wash away years of anger and pain.

Andrew Murray was correct when he wrote, "We must begin to believe that God, in the mystery of prayer, has entrusted us with a force that can move the Heavenly world, and can bring its power down to earth."[1]

Any information the Holy Spirit gives is impregnated with knowledge. It is amazing to be with a person and perceive in a moment's time exactly where to concentrate your prayer. You don't have to know everything yourself, because the Holy Spirit is perfectly accurate in His understanding of human need. This is very freeing! As you become open to the biblical principle of revelation and dare to act upon it in faith, you will not only hear the voice of God, you will see results. Hebrews 11:6 states, "And without faith it is impossible to please Him, for he who comes to God must believe that He is and that He is a rewarder of those who seek Him." The gifts of the Holy Spirit, including discernment of spirits, will begin to infuse new life into your prayer ministry by revealing these areas of need so that you can minister more effectively to people. Will you make mistakes? Yes, it is fairly certain that you will make mistakes, but with practice, you will become more accurate in your ministry of prayer. Be patient with yourself as you learn, and believe that the Holy Spirit is with you to counsel and instruct you. Thousands of lay Christians on our mission trips to Brazil have learned how to pray according to the principles I am sharing with you in this book. The testimonies are endless of how their prayer ministries have been changed and empowered. They simply dared to believe that the Holy Spirit would speak to them in light of the Word and then stepped out in faith to try to be a blessing to someone else. The fruit over the years is immeasurable. If there were no fruit, I would not be writing this book. But the fruit confirms that there is something powerful in what I am sharing with you on these pages.

In the following chapters we will take a detailed look at each one of these four roots one by one, and how they are formed and expressed in the life of a man, woman, or child. As you read each section, you will begin to understand yourself and others in your life more clearly. And it all starts with seeing need the way God sees it.

4

Spiritual Need: The Root of Rejection of Self

Once someone becomes a Christian, he or she is called to be a witness of God's redemptive love. If we do not know and embrace God's love in a personal way, we are not able to grow in that love or minister it to others. This causes us to be wounded as human beings and ineffective as witnesses. The root of rejection of self minimizes, suppresses, and belittles the person. It discourages someone from knowing that he or she has worth and value. Rejection keeps us from realizing God's love for us. There are many Christians who fail to receive God's unconditional, agape love. Though sincere in their faith, they lack spiritual confidence in themselves and in the Lord's ability to deliver them from past and present sins and traumas. This keeps them from growing in faith. It hinders them from reaching their potential in life and from becoming a blessing to others.

From Where Does Rejection of Self Come?

Rejection is a spiritual need, but the root of rejection is created as an individual is rejected by other people: family members, peers, or authority figures. Rejection comes through those who have access to a person's trust and confidence, such as a father or mother or brothers and sisters. Rejection is something that is induced. It is not innate. In other words, it is not something a person just has with no cause. No one chooses to be rejected. It is forced upon someone. I have ministered to children as young as five years of age who have felt rejected in school. An unwanted child can feel rejection from the mother even in the womb. The induction of rejection at an early age creates a precedent that can last a lifetime. A single incident that left a scar of rejection can be remembered forty years later if it is not dealt with.

All of us experience rejection many times in our lives. However, the root of rejection is created in a person when the experiences of rejection become so oppressive that they distort and obscure a healthy relationship with God. The person finds it nearly impossible to consistently believe that she is truly loved by God. Deep rejection by a parent causes feelings of inadequacy within a child that will eventually become the emotional norm. As the child grows, the voice of accusation becomes more familiar and prevalent than the voice of acceptance. The message of worthlessness or low self-esteem can take root in a child's thought processes at a very early age, affecting virtually every area of development, including personality, spirituality, health, and sexuality. All of this interferes with the person's ability to feel accepted and secure in God's love. A pattern of negative self-perception becomes firmly established and remains until it is dealt with by someone who knows how to pray.

When I first came to the United States from Brazil, communication with others was very difficult. I could not understand the language.

I felt totally out of sync with others. I knew that I looked and acted differently than those around me. It was terrible. There were many days when I sat by myself at the high school cafeteria in Madison, Florida, hoping someone—anyone—would speak to me. I had come from a strong Methodist family in Brazil. When I left Brazil, my father had said to me, "Son, you are under the prophetic call of God, blessed of God, and saved by the grace of God." But in those days at Madison High, I felt as if all the prophetic blessing, and maybe even my salvation, was taken from me. The rejection from others was wearing me thin.

Eventually, I even stopped going to church. For a period of time, it was like my faith went cold. I attended school and went to my job at the Shell gas station across from the Baptist church, but my relationship with God almost disappeared. Because I was rejected, I began rejecting God in my life. Interestingly enough, the rejection came from peers, as they became more important than life itself to me. The ladies of the First United Methodist Church saved me from deeper damage as they began to reach out to me with love. Somehow, their love began to compensate for the rejection I was experiencing at school, and I started to feel at least some sense of belonging. I joined a fraternity on the campus of North Florida Junior College, and those young men also took me in. Now little Ricardo was covered by his big brothers! Even though I was raised in a strong Christian faith, the behavior of others deeply affected my life, and nearly shipwrecked my faith.

When praying for young people, you should look for these traits of rejection. Concentrate on family conflicts. A teenager navigating our school systems, with all of the bullying and the negativity that abounds in social media, can develop a root of rejection that will downsize his or her personal worth for many years to come. When praying for others with this basic need of rejection, the point is not to condemn the person or people (mother, father, peers, etc.) who did the rejecting. Your job is not about placing blame. It is about bringing the specific cause of the pain and rejection to light, so that you can pray with accuracy. Sensitivity as to how the root of rejection was formed is critically important to the success of your prayer. Your understanding of the basic need of the person is enough for the Holy Spirit to direct you how to pray accurately without condemning anyone in your prayer. The Holy Spirit is not eager to condemn anyone! He is present to heal and restore the person who has suffered from rejection for so many years.

Rejection of self is often created when one is raised in a home where rejection has also characterized the life of the mother or father. A parent who was abused and unloved himself, may in turn abuse and reject his child. A root of rejection can develop when a child is exposed to sexual aberrations or improprieties. The strongest form of rejection of self comes out of incest. When a person experiences acute rejection such as incest or sexual abuse, this can change his or her personality, branding him or her with an attitude of rejection for life. In looking at the biblical commandments, the Lord is very clear regarding sin within family and self-worth. For example, Exodus 20:17 says, "You shall not covet your neighbor's wife." Likewise, Deuteronomy 27:22 says, "Cursed is he who lies with his sister, the daughter of his father or of his mother." What do we learn about the heart of God in these prohibitions of the law? Each of them pertains to personal rejection among family members and those who live within community. God understands human beings. Our sins against another human being can create a deep problem of rejection, which will affect that person for life.

The Void Inside

Any distortion of love interferes with the discovery of God's love for us. The root of rejection of self turns one inward toward self instead of toward God. The individual with a root of rejection feels a void inside and seeks to fill that void through various means, even illegitimate means. Rejection compels a man or woman to feed the hunger for God with other sorts of behaviors and substances, sometimes causing him or her to use other people for personal benefit. For example, a girl who grows up without a father or the influence of a godly man may seek attention from men in inappropriate ways—using her body in an effort to gain acceptance from men. A man who is addicted to pornography is often trying to fill the void that has been created in his life because of rejection. Since he is not confident and cannot seem to experience intimate relationship with his heavenly Father, he turns to external, false relationships. Failure to realize and believe in God's love leads one to a life of emptiness, where genuine love is replaced by lust. The result of trying to fill the void within can be a spiral into all sorts of addictions and complications, producing even more damage to the self-esteem and causing even further rejection within the family.

Identity

It is interesting to note that what creates a root of rejection in one may have little effect upon another in the same family, or may be experienced in a different way. For example, a young boy loses his father and begins to be dominated by an overbearing mother. His identity suffers, perhaps resulting in effeminacy. This young man may begin to seek acceptance and attention from other men in order to fill the vacuum created by the absence of the father. This is, of course, not always the case. A younger brother may respond in a completely different way to the absence of the father. Each individual responds differently, and the damage may be minimized because of the loving presence of other family members and friends.

A healthy identity is one that is tied up in God. When we know who God is and are sure of His love for us, then we know who we are!

However, one who has a root of rejection experiences a crisis because his identity is tied up in self rather than in Christ. Sometimes we encounter people who are even deeply confused about their gender roles. However, the behavior of masculine women and effeminate men is not necessarily indicative of homosexuality or immorality, but more an indicator of the root of rejection. It is the responsibility of followers of Jesus Christ to see past the consequences and to learn to minister to the pain that lies at the root of such complex problems.

Those rejected by family members experience compounded rejection. Compounded rejection is when the person feels the pain of his or her own rejection in the context of many other rejection issues that prevail within the family. Not only does the individual feel rejected, but the rejection seems to be part of the family line. The father and grandfather or mother and grandmother whose inability to love and care properly for the child because they were unloved themselves will tremendously influence a child. This person will, in essence, say, "Since I have been rejected by my own family, since I do not have a way to know who I really am, I will express myself by the way I feel and by who appears to accept me."

Sexuality

Sexual perversions represent an extreme attempt to overcome rejection. The rejected individual who is seeking to fill a void of love may participate in sexual perversions. These behaviors yield a temporary and false sense of belonging and acceptance but can never satisfy the need for genuine love. When rejection is at this level, you will see an accentuated leaning toward sexual aberrations. This is not simple lust or a desire to experience something new, but rather a strong current enticing a person to become captive in a lifestyle that is far outside of the norm. A circle of relationships develops, which is made up of other rejected persons—all seeking expression of their sexuality in order to satisfy a longing. You find these deeply rejected individuals desperately trying to get their needs met in one another. True and lasting loving relationships will never come out of rejection. Rejection distorts the ability to identify and seek after genuine love rather than false love, since all it does is feed self. Selfish relationships will not satisfy or endure.

Self-Esteem

Rejection robs us of self-esteem, leading us to thought processes that are not Christ-centered. These thought processes cause us to think less of ourselves and blind us to our worth in the kingdom of God. Feelings of insecurity and inferiority convince the rejected person that he or she is not as good as everyone else and therefore not worthy of God's love. These feelings of insecurity naturally lead one to loneliness, self-pity, despair, timidity, ineptness, shyness, and inadequacy.

In order to cope with these feelings, the rejected person may learn at an early age to escape into indifference, becoming passive and indecisive. Some may try to find their escape in food, alcohol, drugs, or gambling. Some may escape via excessive sleeping, excessive exercise, or TV watching. All of these behaviors, in the end, do not satisfy and only serve to intensify the feelings of worthlessness.

The fear of further rejection may turn a person toward self so that he begins to pamper and indulge himself. He may display distorted thinking in relation to his own importance in his home, job, church, or community in order to make himself feel better. This is only a facade to hide his insecurity with ego so that others will believe he is sufficient, important, and free of problems. There may be a tendency for him to tell a bigger story or dominate a conversation to protect himself from the painful inner feeling that he doesn't measure up to the expectations of others.

Passivity

Have you ever met someone who just cannot make up her mind, who cannot seem to make a simple decision and then follow through on that decision? One of the major causes of indecision is passivity of the mind. When rejection has put roots down into one's life, passivity can take over. Webster's Dictionary defines passivity as follows: "Inactive, but acted upon; receiving impressions from external agents; offering no resistance." Mental passivity is inactive, unresponsive behavior to circumstances that require personal responsibility and action. It is lethargy of the mind (see Ephesians 4:17–19). A passive mind is filled with hesitation, lack of concentration, and sometimes poor memory with no justifiable cause.

The passive person is one whose mind is open to allow any thought to come through it without resistance. The passive mind often accepts lies as truth. Most people under passivity are vulnerable to the control of others through manipulation, intimidation, or domination. The passive individual is always looking for definition from someone else. Accepting this control by others paralyzes the person's progress in life.

Conversely, an active mind takes responsibility for changes that must be made in attitude or lifestyle. The passive mind simply takes the position that God will work everything out one way or the other. The active mind understands that God works with us in our reality as we obey His commandments and move according to His will. The passive mind just waits for reality to change. The passive individual is one who often dreams but seldom sees those dreams come to pass in reality.

The passive mind is blinded to the Word of God. It is a reprobate mind, not able to hear and act upon what the Holy Spirit is saying because the word is not real to them. The ambivalent thought processes of the passive mind take on greater validity than what Scripture says regarding a situation. Romans 1:28 speaks to this: "And just as they did not see fit to acknowledge God any longer, God gave them over to a depraved mind, to do those things which are not proper." An active mind accomplishes much and is fruitful in the course of a lifetime, while the passive mind may fail to accomplish some of the simplest tasks and basic goals in life.

Passivity is a derivative of rejection, and the ramifications are many. When the thought processes freeze in the mind, one becomes almost paralyzed. The dreams, the goals, and the call may never materialize because the mind of the servant is iced in place. A passive conscience is a state of stagnation, not responsive to sound reasoning or the efforts of others to motivate. The passive conscience cannot seem to hear truth and cannot take appropriate action as to what should be done. A passive conscience is self-seeking. It creates a false reality, and the voice of God is adjusted and distorted to fit that reality.

In spiritual life, one of the most essential aspects of growth is the ability to reach God when we need His help and mercy. The human spirit thrives on striving and reaching for the best at the worst hour in life. When we watch a basketball tournament, it is thrilling to see players reaching into the depths of their souls, pulling air into their lungs for one more run, one more basket to win the game. However, the passive spirit is uninvolved in the fourth quarter of life when the deciding basket will make it or break it for many.

In your ministry, you will meet people trapped by a passive spirit. Most of them are overwhelmed by a lack of incentive, resulting in no personal growth, year after year. Their spirits are self-seeking and powerless when it comes to the battle of life. They cannot sing, they cannot cry, they cannot dance, they cannot pray, they cannot rejoice. Passivity is destructive—it is not a benign condition—and it robs God of the glory due Him from the life of someone whom He created.

It is easy to detect a passive spirit. Passivity is obvious in the body. You will easily observe idleness, a passive voice, a passive walk, and a passive posture. How often I have watched people coming to the altar for prayer, their very bodies speaking of desperation and defeat: body slumped forward, shoulders lowered, feet dragging, eyes focused on the floor, and hands limp. The root of rejection of self is not hard to miss.

This sight is unforgettable to anyone who loves to pray with accuracy. All you have to do is to open your mouth and let God love someone through you!

When praying for someone who is rejected, pay attention to passivity in any form. For some rejected persons, passivity becomes part of the grid of life. Rejection is the root; passivity is the fruit! When you pray, connect the dots. As you pray for the passive spirit, there are many words you can use to address the bondage. Consider these: hopelessness, heaviness, listlessness, dejection, pouting, escape, and withdrawal. Within the passive spirit, you will find loss of free will, loss of self-control, deceptive thoughts, an idle body, false pride, mental delusion, false wisdom, and a darkened mind. Keep in mind, the root here is rejection. Interpreting these expressions of rejection in the passive person will help you formulate a powerful and effective weapon of prayer, which can set the individual free.

I met a local pastor who was losing all joy in life due to the demands on his ministry. When we began our time of prayer, he spoke of his burdens, his eyes dull and his voice dragging. His speech was so slow that before he finished two sentences, I had already heard everything. Passivity is easily discerned through the demeanor of a person. I prayed him up, and not down. He needed to be set free from rejection and join the battle again!

Withdrawal

The root of rejection brings a spirit of heaviness, including gloom, despondency, defeatism, and sometimes even total withdrawal from reality. Moodiness often characterizes the life of those with a root of rejection. The rejected soul tends to withdraw from reality and substitute his or her perception for reality. Daydreaming, pretension, fantasy, and unreality lead one to delusions about self, God, others, and circumstances. These delusions can even lead to feelings of paranoia, as the person with a root of rejection begins to feel that others are out to cause him mental, spiritual, or physical harm.

Many fight a downward spiral into depression without being able to identify a cause, possibly leading them to thoughts of suicide. One of the most prevalent aspects of rejection is depression, which can paralyze someone's mental activity. The question for you is this: If you desire to pray with accuracy, how do you approach such serious threats to someone's life? We must believe in the overwhelming power of prayer! The greatest miracle of prayer is that when God speaks, He has already fulfilled His Word. When you hear from God, you must believe that He has already done that which He has revealed to you.

Throughout these forty-five years of prayer ministry, the Lord has done many powerful things. It would take several books to tell you all that I have seen Him perform in countless lives. Praying with accuracy is not only possible; it brings eternal results!

Healing of Rejection of Self

When self is in control, there is seldom much of a spiritual life. The root of rejection causes one to focus on self, which totally interferes with a prayer life and an active relationship with God. Remember that rejection keeps a man or woman from realizing God's love and their true identity in Him. It keeps the individual from being an effective witness and a conduit of God's love to others. When one is consumed with self, it is difficult to see the needs of others. Rejection is broken and healed in one's life when the person discovers his identity in a loving Father who deeply cares for him. Wholeness is attained when one's emotions are brought into line with the powerful reality of the love of God.

As Christians, we must first point people to God's love, and then let the Holy Spirit reveal where they are in their view of themselves. Rejection in most cases began much earlier than we may think. Some individuals were not welcomed into the world at all. They were mistreated in the womb or were rejected shortly after birth, and today they are trying to find meaning and hope for their existence.

Only Jesus Christ can bring healing in these cases. That is why prayer here must be specific and to the point. When the Holy Spirit begins to reveal someone's in-depth need, He will point toward a time, a place, a person, or a unique situation that caused the person to feel the way he or she does. The Holy Spirit will speak to this moment as if He knows all about this individual, for indeed He does. Remember that God created the human being in front of you and will carefully take care of him or her.

As we pray for this individual, the root of the problem is rejection, so we speak directly to that root. We do not have to analyze, become emotional, or shout. As we speak the words in prayer, we are simply partnering with the Holy Spirit in doing His work.

Application

Here is a prayer for a man who was rejected by his mother from the moment he was born:

Dear God, heal my brother from the thought of rejection that is entrenched in his soul. In the most powerful name of Jesus Christ, I stand against every legal right of Satan against you, my brother, and against your family. I speak against all suggestions, lies, and acts that have diminished you and created a feeling of not being accepted, loved, and valued. I stand against all things that have been said and done to you to minimize, accuse, and condemn you as a person. I speak to your heart and I ask Christ to heal your emotions today. I declare that you are loved, accepted, and so precious to the Father that He sent His Son to bear shame and rejection in your place on the cross. I set you free from all rejection in the name of Jesus Christ. Amen.

5

Spiritual Need: The Root of Rejection of God

Rejection of God (rebellion) is the crafting of a thought, object, or idea and setting it above the knowledge of God. The root of rejection of God separates one from the Savior because faith in Him is crippled. It is being in opposition to almighty God by refusing to relate to Him by faith.

When I had finished two master's degrees, one in divinity and one in speech communication, and an associate bachelor degree in journalism from the University of Georgia, I was spiritually bankrupt. My mind had been away from God and His ways. I couldn't care less about going to church, and my weekends of traveling to sing or even to preach consisted of pure entertainment. Since my mind was in opposition to the Lord, my ministry had nothing to offer anyone else. I was in rebellion against God.

Rejection of God takes place in the thought processes and is therefore a matter of the mind. One who is rejecting God is not submitted to Him. The person is deceived into following his own will or the will of others rather than following the Lord. The will of the individual in rebellion has already been established in spite of God's voice, or because the voice of the Holy Spirit has been drowned out by the noise of the intellect. The tendency is to either move ahead of God or stay behind Him in disobedience as we hear our own minds louder than the voice of the Holy Spirit.

Paul writes to the church in Corinth about this spiritual problem of rejection of God (rebellion) in 2 Corinthians 10:3–6:

> For though we walk in the flesh, we do not war according to the flesh, for the weapons of our warfare are not of the flesh, but divinely powerful for the destruction of fortresses [concepts entrenched in the mind]. We are destroying speculations and every lofty thing raised up against the knowledge of God, and we are taking every thought captive to the obedience of Christ, and we are ready to punish all disobedience, whenever your obedience is complete.

Notice that the text here is all about the mind. Rebellion toward God creates a "fortress"—concepts firmly established in the mind— that are raised up, or given more importance, than the intimate, revealed knowledge of God. The text is also about obedience. Obedience can only come when you trust God more than you trust yourself, and you become willing for His will to supersede your will. This is not easy for one who trusts in his own intellect and reasoning more than the relationship and guidance that can be accessed only by a living faith in God (see also 1 Corinthians 2:10–14).

Expressions of Rejection of God

Pride

Theology that produces no fruit has no power. A steady diet of religious analysis and discourse can actually create a serious lack of faith.

Those who are "holding to a form of godliness, although they have denied its power" (2 Tim. 3:5a), as they endlessly practice and defend religious exegetics, offend God. In pride, they prefer to know *about* God instead of pursuing a vital relationship *with* Him. Rejection of God can manipulate a person into defending ideas that are opposed to the Word of God but support the popular reasoning or agenda of the moment. The person has the idea that satisfaction comes by knowing more than others and always being right. However, spiritual matters cannot be received or reasoned with the mind alone. To find Him, we must humble ourselves and admit that He is God and we are not.

Isaiah 55:8–9 puts it this way: "'For My thoughts are not your thoughts, nor are your ways My ways,' declares the LORD. 'For as the heavens are higher than the earth, so are My ways higher than your ways, and My thoughts than your thoughts.'"

Rejection of God (rebellion) is tied up with pride. The person has a driving desire to appear superior, more knowledgeable, and more learned than others. He is often unwilling to receive the Word or ministry from those he considers beneath him. This goes directly against Jesus' exhortation in Matthew 11:29: "Take My yoke upon you, and learn from Me, for I am gentle and humble in heart, and you will find rest for your souls."

I met a pastor who struggled with faith, his ideas of God, and especially the divinity of Jesus Christ. He had extensive theological knowledge but he had no peace in his mind about Christ. For more than twenty years he had suffered and struggled with spiritual things, rationalizing to the point of no return. One night on a mission trip I was translating for him as he preached in a church in Rio de Janeiro. He was speaking on all the colors of the rainbow. He equated blue to life's dark days, where loneliness affects your mornings and blows dark clouds over your evenings. Red, he said, was the point of crisis, which comes to us as we journey this pilgrim path. Black was related to depression and white was about peace. He went on and on, speaking a lot of meaningless words. This was not the living, pulsing, powerful Word of God!

I looked at the congregation and realized they, of course, were receiving nothing through this discourse about colors in the rainbow. Now this was a Portuguese-speaking Brazilian congregation; they could not understand what my English-speaking brother was saying. So I simply began translating his English words into Portuguese another way! "My" sermon spoke about blue being full of doubt and fear of the future. I said that Christ alone brings peace regarding one's future. I said that red is the color of His blood shed on the cross of Calvary, where our Savior gave His life for each one of us. White was related to salvation, the washing away of all our sin, and sanctification by His grace and mercy. I proclaimed that Christ alone brings fullness of life to anyone who does not have it. I made an invitation for those who wanted to receive Jesus Christ to come forward.

To my brother's amazement, and mine, everyone came forward for salvation that evening! As my friend prayed humbly for those who came, I told him that his sermon convicted everyone of the person of Jesus Christ. This was the straw that broke all rebellion in his mind. This is what he had been searching and longing for over the duration of his entire ministry. Never before had he seen the fruit of transformed souls as a result of his preaching, even though he had hungered to experience just that. Floods of tears began to flow from his eyes as he prayed for everyone that night. After that evening he was a changed man. He preached the whole week, and hundreds came forward to receive Christ. He preached without notes, speaking freely about the Savior. His rebellion, expressed in his own lofty thoughts and meaningless discourse raised up above the true knowledge of God, had been soundly defeated! He had tasted of life in the Spirit and did not wish to go back.

When you hear a sermon solely based on human skill and intellect, you are observing mind idolatry at work. Many of us prepare and do research, especially if we are students of the Word, and this is good. However, when rebellion is operating at the core of someone, you do not hear the Savior in his message, only the speaker and his eloquent words. You do not hear the living Word, only the prideful thoughts of the individual. It may be delivered with enthusiasm and wit, but the Holy Spirit is not present. God is actually not welcome in the environment. This is an expression of the rejection of God. It is offensive to Him and quenches all movement of the Holy Spirit.

It takes only a moment to observe rejection of God (rebellion), which is enough to provide everything you need in order to pray a biblical prayer for that individual. Rebellion is the easiest root to detect, even when the person is not living a blatantly rebellious lifestyle. Sometimes the expression is obvious, such as a manner of dress or a hairstyle. Rebellion can be expressed by a haughty look, a proud walk, or a furrowed brow, indicating that the mind is racing to analyze everything being said. It can be revealed through statements of doubt about the holy things of God.

Simply the voice and manner of how a person speaks gives extensive information about what is going on in the person's mind. In the Gospels, Jesus took in the words of Jairus, the touch of the woman with the issue of blood, and the voice of blind Bartimaeus and knew instantly who they all were. When you have the intention to really hear the person in need and to hear God in those moments, you, too, will discern what is there. How do you deal with a senior member of your church who is constantly registering complaints about what happens on a Sunday morning? How do you minister to a member of your leadership who is continuously debating religious minutiae with others? How about the choir director whose music does not relate to the membership of the church, yet she refuses to adapt, insisting that it is her way or the highway? Do you know how to approach a person in such a quagmire of rebellion? When the root is not addressed, the situation will continue to deteriorate. It is imperative that we learn to discern and deal with rebellion in the midst of the church. Rebellion is rampant, and leaders who have this problem will do much damage and stifle the healthy growth of others in the church if rebellion is not confronted.

How can healing begin? You can be in love with Jesus and never receive His Spirit. You can talk about forgiveness and never feel forgiven. It is a matter of the heart. When someone rejects God, it is premeditated. This person has already established rigid dogmas and postures regarding theological issues, and, in the process, is closed off to the conviction and sanctifying work of the Holy Spirit. This person has a serious spiritual need. Healing begins when the heart asks for help.

I met a pastor who had a career of thirty years in ministry. In truth, he knew that he had never really accomplished anything extraordinary in all of his years of service. He felt empty inside, and though he wanted to see people impacted for the kingdom, few were. In his heart, he even knew that many of his ideologies were against God. Though he didn't know what to do to change himself, he admitted that he was tired of it. In a prayer of surrender, the root was identified. I remember it well; I prayed, "Father, this is Your servant who has served his own mind for years now. Today, he has decided to surrender his rebellious mind to You. No more doubting, no more rationalizing, no more compromising with faith, no more resisting the Holy Spirit of God! No more!" I heard from this pastor one year later, and he shared that people were coming to faith in the Lord Jesus Christ as never before. God was speaking through him, finally! When the heart of someone is open just a little bit to the Holy Spirit, God can get in there and perform wonders.

Perfectionism

Another expression of rejecting God is perfectionism. The person with a root of rebellion often tries to compensate for her lack of faith by overdoing and performing. She establishes goals, which are generally unattainable, even for herself. This creates stress and fear as she continually strives for perfection, but ultimately fails. Perfectionism is a form of fear, rooted in idolatry. Eventually, attaining perfection becomes more important than life, others, and even the Lord Himself. We must remember that perfection is reserved for God only, as only God is perfect. The person may be dressed impeccably, be obsessed about body issues and cleanliness and order, and devote huge amounts of time and energy to maintaining certain standards of excellence when there really is no call for it. Perfectionism is a false dictator that robs one of experiencing all of God's love and blessings with joy.

In perfectionism, the fear that surrounds one's mind is related to the idolatry of one's own ideas and fears. Religious perfectionism becomes legalism, wherein a believer attempts to please God through adhering to codes of conduct and religious rules. This deceived believer is attempting to achieve self-righteousness through law instead of enjoying the intimacy of relationship with God and dependence upon His lavish grace. When a person rejects God's perfection as being sufficient and tries to establish his or her personal perfection instead, it is not only legalistic, it is behavior rooted in rebellion. The only lasting remedy is to go to the core need in these cases, if we are truly going to help someone. Debating the behaviors, the beliefs, and the place of the law will not help. This person needs to repent of exalting his or her thoughts and ways over the revelation of the gospel of peace in Christ Jesus.

Hypersensitivity

Hypersensitivity to others and self is a form of fear. The desire for perfection causes one to have an exaggerated self-awareness, which leads to fears of all kinds: fear of man, fear of finances, fear of failure, and fear of the future. The drive to control and manipulate people and situations instead of trusting God arises out of this fear—and the result is worry, anxiety, stress, and apprehension. Hypersensitivity can cause illness of the mind and body. You cannot live peacefully in an environment where everything and everyone must constantly adapt to your desires and fears. This kind of overblown sensitivity brings bondage. It kills joy and spiritual growth. The hypersensitive person may become reserved and introverted. She may be so self-absorbed and concerned about what people think of her, that she becomes unapproachable and also unable to reach out in love to others. In the end, this leaves a person feeling very isolated and unfulfilled.

All of this may sound like a relational problem, but it is a really a spiritual problem. This is because the core issue lies between the person and God. The person is pushing God away. Once healing begins there, in the relationship with God, relationships with other people will also begin to change. Are you beginning to see why a biblical perspective of human need, coupled with revelation from the Holy Spirit, is so important?

Reasoning over Revelation

"But I am afraid that, as the serpent deceived Eve by his craftiness, your minds will be led astray from the simplicity and purity of devotion to Christ" (2 Cor. 11:3). The Bible tells us that it is in the simple things of faith that we find strength and peace. We reject God with our minds when we idolize the pursuit of knowledge as our main source of strength. Prayer is of the spirit, not an exercise of the mind, and it operates through the power of revelation that comes only from God. One, therefore, rejects God when he or she allows the mind to take over that which is only accessed by faith. Reasoning can be as deadly as a poisonous snake.

Philippians 4:7 states, "And the peace of God, which surpasses all comprehension, will guard your hearts and your minds in Christ Jesus." Peace surpasses comprehension! In other words, if you have the peace of God in your heart through complete faith in Him, you don't need to understand and comprehend everything! Our Lord does not expect us to know and explain every theological enigma. What He is looking for in His servants, more than anything else, is a living faith.

Here is a biblical example. Mark 2:5–11 tells the story of Jesus healing the paralytic: "And Jesus seeing their faith said to the paralytic, 'Son, your sins are forgiven.' But some of the scribes were sitting there and reasoning in their hearts, 'Why does this man speak that way? He is blaspheming; who can forgive sins but God alone?'"

In this passage, Jesus healed the lame man who was lowered through the roof of the house in Capernaum. The human intellect of the scribes could not conceive of the words spoken by Jesus, "Son, your sins are forgiven," so they began to reason and debate scriptures and the law in their minds. Jesus simply asked them, "Why are you reasoning?" (v. 8). He knew that the scribes were Jews of intellect and training who functioned mentally, but were spiritually empty.

Since rejection of God primarily takes place in your intellect, this is a scary concept. We are taught all of our lives to build up our minds, to be educated, and to think things through in order to approach life and to solve life's puzzles and challenges. Yes, God has created our minds and how the mind works is a marvel of His creation. We are made in His image, having been given by our Creator amazing abilities of intellect, communication, creativity, memory, and so much more. Nonetheless, we are rejecting the Lord when we allow ourselves and our minds to be elevated above and take the place of revelation from the very one who created us. He is higher than His creation!

It is regrettable that so much of what we read in biblical commentaries does not come by revelation from the Holy Spirit. The thoughts and contributions of men can enhance our understanding, but these never were intended by the Lord to take the place of hearing directly from Him, or to be the main source for our preaching of the Word. Rejecting God is demonstrated by one who only hears what appeals to the mind. As you pray, your desire to hear God has to exceed your desire to hear from your own mind. Faith has to take its place.

Some of us think so much that it would take a spiritual hurricane for us to be able to hear from God. For many years, I preached sermons that were filled only with what came from my mind. It was not until I humbled myself and gave revelation from the Holy Spirit a chance that my entire ministry changed forever.

Application

Here is an example of a prayer for someone bound up in his or her mind, having difficulty hearing from God:

Our Father, I come against all rejection of You. I speak to all thoughts that rise above the knowledge of God. I take authority over all unbelief, over all fear, and over all intellectualism that belittles the work of the cross. I take authority over self-will and striving for perfection apart from the blood of Jesus Christ. In the authority of Jesus Christ and His precious blood, I sever all relationships with the occult and the conjuring of thoughts that block Your presence. In Your precious and holy name, I reprimand all thoughts that would mock the person of Jesus Christ and His work of salvation on the cross. I take authority over the rule and reign of all rationalization, ego, and pride in this child of God. In the name of Jesus Christ, I stand against all communion with minds that have been turned over to wickedness in suppressing the truth of God. From this moment forward, in the authority given to me by God, I set you free to live and experience a life of childlike faith in the grace of God through Jesus Christ, our Lord. Amen.

———————————————

6

Relational Need: The Root of Unforgiveness

When Jesus spoke the words in Mark 12:31, "You shall love your neighbor as yourself," He confirmed a basic human need. People have difficulties with other people, and this affects their lives as a whole. These conflicts must be resolved so that a child of God may function properly in life. Unforgiveness destroys the peace that should thrive in the heart of every Christian. Unforgiveness creates suspicion, paranoia, anger, discord, envy, and strife.

The authors of the Old Testament refer to the basic root of unforgiveness when the law condemns behaviors such as mistreating the Jews, dishonoring parents, defrauding or stealing from your neighbor, or taking advantage of the blind (see Genesis 27:29; Deuteronomy 27:16–18). The commandments regarding mistreating widows, orphans, and aliens also involve attitudes toward others (see Deuteronomy 27:19). These citations indicate that in the heart of God, He holds specific parameters as to how He wants us to relate to others. These Scripture references to offending persons of value, offending parents, and taking advantage of the most vulnerable amongst us are profoundly important to the heart of the Lord. God is telling us that this relational issue of unforgiveness is dealt with strongly in His Word, and deserves our undivided attention.

[Side note: Concerning the word *aliens*. We are living at a time when immigration to America is under contentious scrutiny and debate. While national security is a critically urgent priority, we must be careful not to estrange aliens altogether. There are always those whom God is sending to America, and the people of God should be the first to care for them and show them the love of Jesus.]

Ministering to the Root of Unforgiveness

The question at this point in our study is: How do you minister to people who are experiencing this relational need of unforgiveness? First, you acknowledge that this is a problem that is common among us. Think of it like this: If God's way of seeing human need divides all of the complexities of our human sins and weaknesses into only two areas, spiritual and relational, then the relational issue of unforgiveness must be very common to man!

All of us have experienced difficulty in dealing with someone within our family, work, or community. Since having discord with others is common to man, how can you discern whether a root of unforgiveness has become the core, or the area of greatest need, in someone's life? Remember that we learned in chapter 2 that your problem is with God (spiritual) or your problem is with others (relational). It seems much easier to recognize someone with a spiritual problem who is rejecting self or God. The relational root of unforgiveness can be more difficult to identify in an individual unless you understand how it is formed and how it is expressed.

Always keep in mind that prayer is an exercise of your spirit more than an exercise of your mind. Let God lead you in how to pray.

Discernment of spirits or any other gift is a movement of the Holy Spirit that points to areas of need. You are not alone in this quest. You are being guided by a mighty God who wants to see you minister powerfully through prayer. He will teach you bit by bit as you depend on Him. Let your ministry begin with a revelation from God. I have been telling you stories throughout this book of what has happened to me during my many years of ministry. I hope you will receive these stories as a testimony of what God has done for me and as an encouragement of what He can do through you!

I was praying for a woman at an Arkansas church in the pastor's office during a revival weekend. As we started to pray, I asked the woman to tell me about her sister, and she began to cry. A broiling feud had been going on for more than five years between the sisters. I suggested that the woman drive that afternoon to the house of her sister, and mend the relationship. She was hesitant at first, but finally agreed to do what the Lord, through me, was instructing her. She and her sister were completely reconciled, but it didn't stop there! Healing of other disputes within the extended family began to spread, and she was very encouraged to see how God was working in the entire family. It was all because she took that first step to let the Lord deal with her own root of unforgiveness.

Notice that it all began by addressing the rancor between two sisters. The core of the unforgiveness will be found to be directed against a single person, and not a whole group of people, even though there may be multiple relationships that have become strained. Begin your prayer by seeking to learn from the Holy Spirit: Where did the pain begin? Who, in the mind of the person you are praying for, is responsible for the greatest pain? You must address the problem from the core—the root.

Biblically speaking, unforgiveness is easy to understand. The discourse between Jesus and Peter in Matthew 18:21–22 gives us a valuable scriptural look at unforgiveness: "Then Peter came and said to Him, 'Lord, how often shall my brother sin against me and I forgive him? Up to seven times?' Jesus said to him, 'I do not say to you, up to seven times, but up to seventy times seven.'"

Jesus Christ himself takes unforgiveness seriously. At the end of the passage in Matthew 18:33–35, Jesus says, "'Should you not also have had mercy on your fellow slave, in the same way I had mercy on you?' And his lord, moved with anger, handed him over to the torturers until he should repay all that was owed him. My heavenly Father will also do the same to you, if each of you does not forgive his brother from your heart.'"

If you read the entire parable, the first slave was willing to be forgiven, but he was not willing to forgive. Jesus told the story to Peter to demonstrate that a forgiving heart both receives forgiveness that is not deserved and gives forgiveness that is not deserved. In the parable the master forgave an enormous, unrepayable debt, which would be equal to millions of dollars by today's standards. In turn, he expected that the servant would follow his example and extend the same compassion to anyone who was indebted to him. Forgiveness must be a two-way street. In this passage the penalty for unforgiveness was that the man was to be handed over to the torturers. This is a hard word! Why is unforgiveness so serious? It is serious because we were created in the image of God. That means we were created to love others and to be loved. To whatever degree we cannot love and receive love, we are broken and our purpose as human beings is put down and diminished. Difficult as it may be at times, you will never be fulfilled and whole unless you are able to live with others in family and in community.

You might be thinking it would be much easier if we could just exist on our own little islands and not have to deal with the sins and faults of other people. Yes, in some ways it certainly would be easier! But our Creator fashioned us to develop, learn, and grow within the context of human relationships. When He said of Adam, "It is not good for the man to be alone" (Gen. 2:18), He was not only referring to our capacity for reproduction. We were designed by our Father to have communion with Him *and* communion with other human beings. It is in our DNA. God wanted a family who would love Him and love one another. It brings Him glory and fulfills His purpose for us. Thus, to forgive and to be forgiven is crucial to living a life with God in His kingdom!

When Jesus said that loving your neighbor fulfills the law, He meant that you actually make your neighbor a part of your life! How can you love your neighbor without engaging with him or her in real life? Sometimes people with unforgiveness hide within a crowd, or even within family. They are physically present, but they have essentially shut out everyone around them. At first, this self-imposed wall may seem to be a place of safety. But as the years go by, it becomes a place of isolation and torture. In the case of unforgiveness, it is this condition that that Lord wants to heal. He wants each of us set free to fulfill the scriptural mandate to "love your neighbor as yourself" (Mark 12:31).

In prayer for unforgiveness, you must engage yourself on several fronts. Here are two things I have learned in my years of praying for people:

1) *The root of unforgiveness has characteristics that are different from those found in the roots of rejection of self and rejection of God.* When you see personality weaknesses, such as timidity and shyness, these traits point toward someone who has been rejected. In unforgiveness, you are looking at different symptoms, such as anger, detachment, unrest, and a critical spirit. Unforgiveness brings a hard demeanor, aloofness, irritability, sadness, and an obstinate and inflexible personality.

It seems that when you are at odds with someone, your very countenance changes. Your joy is taken from you. Your smile is not present, and the facial expression is dulled. Unforgiveness literally changes the way you look. I have never met someone harboring deep unforgiveness who sleeps well or genuinely enjoys being with people, because they don't trust anyone. Some individuals are so entrenched in unforgiveness that they defend it; they live it as if it is the order of life. I have never seen unforgiving people to be carefree. Most of them are conflicted, justifying their behavior by trying to keep an outward appearance of everything being perfectly fine, even though their thoughts are filled with frustration and turmoil.

2) *The root of unforgiveness robs a person of friendship.* People who cannot forgive decay faster due to the lack of friends. Friendship with others is something that you win by being real. Human beings want to belong, to be loved, and to be accepted. Unforgiveness takes the tender part out of you and causes you to become difficult to live with. Thus, the assurance of having true friends is missing in the life of anyone whose heart cannot forgive. You become a loner, with walls around you. It seems that no one understands you, and indeed they do not, because you keep the real you hidden. You trust no one. The few friends you do have come around only out of duty, obligation, or pity. Because of unforgiveness, your approach to relationships is selfish and false—creating a barrier between you and others.

You are afraid to be open and vulnerable, so the real you cannot come out and become part of life. The person filled with unforgiveness is isolated from experiencing the joys of having true community and intimate friendships.

Once while preaching in Kentucky, my attention was drawn to a woman in the congregation who was so full of resentment toward another person that no one would even sit close to her. They could actually feel her pain and anger and it caused them to draw back. Unforgiveness creates a specific atmosphere. Simply observing this atmosphere and these characteristics in someone will help you become accurate in your prayer for someone trapped in the bondage of unforgiveness.

Expressions of Unforgiveness

We see many problems with teenagers acting out in anger toward the family. Parents using cruel, harsh words or even physical violence with their teenagers has become common these days. Exodus 21:15 forbids children striking or attacking their parents. However, a child who is rejected, abused, or betrayed by a parent may react strongly out of their hurt and anger by lashing out at the parent verbally or physically. When a fifteen-year-old has endured years of harshness and verbal abuse, they need to find a way to respond to their inner pain. In our society today, teens are reacting to the years of rejection and neglect. For some, the root of rejection of self (discussed in chapter 3) is formed and then characterizes the child's life. For others a deep volcano of unforgiveness begins to mount. In a matter of years, a root of unforgiveness is so resident in his or her life that a wide chasm forms between the parent and the child. It is as if the parent lives in a totally different world than the child.

When praying for parents and children, you must pay close attention to family unrest and feelings of unforgiveness. The right words in prayer for someone with a root of unforgiveness can unlock a puzzle that has enslaved a person or family for generations. If the root is unforgiveness, the Holy Spirit will direct you to the exact place to begin your prayer. You are reading this book in order to learn how to minister through accurate prayer. I guarantee you, when there is a human need as important as unforgiveness within a family, the Holy Spirit will speak very strongly to you, revealing exactly how you are to pray.

Extended Grief

I am now going to tell you a secret that will help you tremendously in your quest to pray with accuracy for hurting people. It has to do with extended grief. You see, extended grief is a product of a relational problem. Unforgiveness is common in situations where the family is broken apart by a significant loss such as separation, divorce, or death. Think of a mother who abandons the family, leaving three small children. You can imagine the grief that these children will experience in a lifetime. All of their achievements and successes are unable to compensate for such an unfulfilled need. The abandonment of a mother is very difficult to forget and to forgive.

Normally, a person moves from grief to healing within about three years. However, when the loss continues to be painfully grieved year after year, even decades in people's lives, something is wrong. This is all too common. You will find extended grief actually encouraged in some churches, almost as a ritual. It is as though the dead are never released to go to their reward and rest, and the living are not released to move on into a new season of life. I ask you: Is it biblical for a mature Christian to deeply mourn a family member for many, many years after his or her death? Is this the will of God for us? Missing and reminiscing about a loved one is totally normal, but what is the cause of wrenching grief that seems to have no end in sight?

The main reason for extended grief that goes far beyond the norm is unforgiveness. When mourning is complicated by unforgiveness, it is prolonged beyond the scope of what is normal and healthy. Even though a grieving individual may experience a certain amount of healing with counseling, they will continue to be trapped in sorrow and grief for many more years if the unforgiveness is not honestly addressed.

Where does the unforgiveness lie? In the aftermath of losing a loved one, we often blame ourselves for any number of perceived wrongs. Perhaps we feel we did not do enough during the last stages of the deceased's life, and we hold onto that guilt. We may feel a certain degree of anger at the one who is gone, blaming him or her for leaving us. We may blame family members for being absent or for certain behaviors during the time of loss. Some of us direct our anger toward God. If there is unresolved unforgiveness and guilt following a loss, the blame must be placed on someone: family members, self, the one who died, or on God Himself. Whatever the case, dealing with the guilt and anger is essential to bringing a person to the place where he or she can eventually resolve the loss, experience healing, and learn to join life again.

How do you pray for someone who is experiencing extended grief? When someone is still deeply connected on a daily basis with someone who has died, he or she will have a depressive, morbid appearance. It is impossible to be in the cemetery day after day and still experience joy and hope regarding life. I cannot count the number of times that I have counseled in a Sunday school room overlooking the church graveyard, looking into the eyes of a saintly Christian woman who is trapped in anger because her deceased husband did not get her permission to die first!

When praying, be aware that many people, especially the elderly, are experiencing extended grief. Keep in mind that this is a relational problem. Thinking this way, you are on biblical ground, and the Holy Spirit will also guide you with much information. Details will surface quickly into your mind. The Holy Spirit concentrates on pain and need. He will move faster than you, helping you to see into the heart of the person in front of you who needs your prayer.

Anger, Envy, and Strife

Unforgiveness produces strife in a family or a relationship. Strife involves contention, arguments, discord, and fighting. These emotional behaviors arise out of conflicts that remain unresolved for a long period of time. The inability to forgive past hurts can cause one's emotions to become easily excited. A person may take out the unforgiveness on others with whom there is no offense, causing those relationships to become strained and unhealthy as well.

A human soul poisoned with unforgiveness can experience emotions of envy and strife so volatile as to affect one's life even to death. Anger and resentment build as lingering memories of past offenses and events continue to influence the present and future. An individual with a root of unforgiveness may live with a feeling of generalized sorrow, making joy a distant thing of the past, with little hope of experiencing it in the future. Unforgiveness as a whole can almost paralyze someone into a passive state of mental inertia. At the same time, outbursts of anger and strife are momentary reactions that erupt and wane—arising from circumstance to circumstance.

When praying about this area of anger, envy, and strife, the goal is to identify a name. The Holy Spirit is very personal in these situations. Simply ask for the name of the one person who caused or who still is causing all the inner torment. Just voicing the name of the person will bring all of the pain to the surface, and you will be able to begin your prayer with pinpoint accuracy. In every situation involving conflict, you will be praying for a soul whose rights have been violated, whose hopes have been crushed, and whose life has been torn apart because of animosity that began with one key person. When the name is cited, then begin to pray from a positive point of view. What does that mean? It means you are to lift up the person who is receiving prayer, not acting as the judge, jury, and executioner of the individual who appears to be the perpetrator. Since the one you are praying for has been deeply affected by another person, it is likely that that very same person may soon become a major player in the healing process. Oh yes! These are the ways of our loving heavenly Father!

Never forget that you are there to pray for restoration, not to condemn. Your objective is to be a conduit of healing. God is the Judge, and you are not. This can be very difficult to do because when you hear what has happened to the hurting person, you tend to take sides. But in prayer you must not take sides. You simply pray, and the Lord does the healing. Think about it this way: the person who caused the greatest pain is also the person who may hold the key to the miracle. When a name comes forth, you can expect to see a breakthrough.

If the one who caused the most pain is still alive, there are many times when the hope is to see the parties come back together. The Lord may use you to facilitate a meeting where they sit down face-to-face and speak forgiveness to one another. Of course, this is not possible or appropriate in all cases. The point is, if you criticize the perpetrator, you are actually closing the door for healing to come through. Remember that the offender is also a child of God who is in need of forgiveness, healing, and restoration. When you look at all of the individuals involved in this scenario of strife, you will find that the perpetrator is a victim of life and as deserving of forgiveness as anyone else.

Accusation

A major indicator of unforgiveness is the accusation of others. Accusation is prideful and consists of judging, blaming, criticizing, and faultfinding. In accusation, unforgiveness begins to crystallize in someone's behavior and his or her entire outlook on life. Having a strong propensity to distrust, suspect, and accuse others places a person in a state of constant loneliness and turmoil. He might claim that all is well, but his face shows a different story. His heart is full of negativity, uneasiness, and unrest.

Often I find myself praying for people who have lost their jobs. Some of them are full of faith and confidence that God is faithful and will provide for them. However, when deep-seated unforgiveness and resentment are present, there is an underlying attitude that life, God, and the world are totally unfair. Issues of resentment, entitlement, and antagonism complicate the crisis. The lack of a job is a small problem, but when such a setback has caused the person's spiritual growth to come to a halt, and the individual seems more interested in placing blame than trusting God, look for unforgiveness.

When someone is accusing another, there is an inner dialogue of judging, blame, suspicion, and faultfinding going on. The mind of the person is constantly filled with these prideful and negative thoughts toward others. The parties here are a million miles away from one another, even though they may be members of the same church or live under the same roof as a family. Prayer that addresses these situations must be carefully constructed. The prayer of accuracy comes into play when you call the issue what it is: accusation. The only way to address these things is to speak under the authority of a higher power, that of Jesus Christ. You cannot merely say that these things are unacceptable in your own opinion. These attitudes and emotions are completely against the Word of God and the holy nature of God. So, pray them out. Pray that they be made void and nullified in the name of Jesus Christ. Lift up the person who is experiencing these emotions and ask the Lord for peace within their heart and within their environment.

Identifying Unforgiveness

Many signs point toward unforgiveness. I have mentioned extended grief, anger, envy, strife, and accusation. Unresolved conflict between human beings drains the soul, just as living without water for days drains the body. It is as if the very skin of a person changes when relationships are in trouble. For some people with a root of unforgiveness, the issue is not necessarily another person who wronged them. A good percentage of individuals I have prayed for have themselves to forgive. Their mistakes, failures, and actions of the past remain in their minds and continue to belittle them in their daily lives.

When you look at someone who has difficulty forgiving, you might see hard lines in the face and shoulders that are tense. Many times you will also see a lack of expression. The person does not respond normally to a smile or a greeting. Not every person you meet will have hard facial lines, but you may experience hardness in his or her voice. Just as someone blinks her eyelids when she is nervous, someone with unforgiveness will often stare and barely move her eyelids. Just as the hands of a farmer show hard work, the hands of an unforgiving person can show more severe damage, as if the constant tension has almost deformed the hands. Unforgiveness can create hardness in the face, hands, demeanor, voice, and movements of an individual.

When praying for someone who has held unforgiveness for a long time, keep in mind that feelings have been hardened and repressed. No one wants to be exposed in such a painful and personal area of life. An unforgiving person is always uncomfortable with the truth. As you pray, you will probably run into extreme discomfort at the thought of even bringing these painful issues to light. The person may adamantly deny that they hold any unforgiveness and claim that they have forgiven all. Therefore, the prayer here must begin with encouraging the person who is receiving prayer. Remember that unforgiveness is a relational condition. Others are involved in the situation. The person may be reluctant to discuss the events or people who are at the center of the offense. But your foremost objective is to identify the person who has caused the deepest hurt. This is possible if you allow the Holy Spirit to give information to you through revelation.

Receiving Forgiveness

Be obedient to the voice of the Holy Spirit. Once when I was praying for a young woman, she denied all of my attempts to deal with the problem of unforgiveness. But the Holy Spirit would not let her go. She acknowledged that she had been in a painful relationship when she was seventeen years of age, and admitted an incident that had broken her heart. The same sort of drama occurred at the age of twenty-five with another person. But then she began to speak emotionally, and it was about the death of someone in her life. As it turned out, it was the death of her child, whom she had aborted. When she realized that God still loved her even after she had done such a terrible thing, and that He would forgive her for past sins, she finally accepted my prayer and received healing in her life.

The individual with a root of unforgiveness finds it difficult to receive forgiveness. Since our entire relationship with Christ is built on our faith in His ability to forgive us and to receive us through grace, that relationship is blocked if we cannot fully receive His forgiveness. Scripture says, "If we confess our sins, He is faithful and righteous to forgive us our sins and to cleanse us from all unrighteousness" (1 John 1:9). When we make a confession of our sins, God promises us that He is faithful to forgive us. Therefore, forgiveness does not depend upon how we feel, but upon receiving God's forgiveness by faith according to His promise in His Word.

To receive the Lord's forgiveness, you must acknowledge that you are fully forgiven. You must offer thanks to God for His grace and forgiveness. You must call yourself forgiven and act as though you are. True forgiveness requires that we forgive ourselves for the choices we have made in life. If we know that God forgives us when we come before Him with a repentant heart, then we must come into agreement with Him and forgive ourselves. The enemy of our souls, who in Revelation 12:10 is called "the accuser of our brethren," will continually tell the believer that he or she cannot be forgiven. But Satan is a liar and this lie must be resisted. Are you going to believe God, who promises to forgive us all our sin if we confess and repent, or are you going to believe the liar? This becomes a choice of the will to believe what God says, rather than believe the devil or even one's own feelings.

Forgiving Others

God is without limit when it comes to forgiveness, and He calls us to be without limit also. Luke 17:4 says, "And if he sins against you seven times a day, and returns to you seven times, saying, 'I repent,' forgive him." Forgiveness requires that one be willing to forgive repeated infractions, which can be very difficult, and goes against our human nature. But the Word is clear: if one is counting how many times he or she forgives someone, he or she is not truly forgiving.

Forgiveness is an expression of love. Andrew Murray wrote, "Our forgiving love toward men is the evidence of God's forgiving love in us. It is a necessary condition of the prayer of faith."[1] Love is a decision; therefore, forgiveness is deciding to love. Being open to love means that you will probably be hurt again because human beings hurt one another. However, once the person in need discovers that forgiveness truly is possible, she will see that being hurt is not as bad as being alone in life, cut off from love and community. Colossians 3:13 exhorts us, "Bear with each other and forgive one another if any of you has a grievance against someone. Forgive as the Lord forgave you" (NIV).

To be able to release others who have wronged us requires that we act out of love, refusing to hold on to resentment. This is not easy. It can be a mighty struggle. Forgiveness is not simply forgetting that wrong has been done. Some wounds are so deep that this would be impossible. We can be healed of the pain, but the act of the insult or the damage has been branded into the mind. Forgiveness takes place when the victim deliberately cancels a debt which is owed by the offending person. Also, anger must be dealt with openly and honestly. Instead of venting it in retaliation, the injured party must confess it in prayer in order to release himself and to set the other party free.

The Holy Spirit begins to reveal the need with a word, and it may be as simple as the word *man, father, sister,* or *mother.* You do not always need to mention names, just relationships. That will be enough to trigger the Holy Spirit to delve right to the core of the need. Pray without fear. If there is a name of a person who is to be voiced in this prayer, get the name of that person. Pray for release, pray for forgiveness, pray for mercy, and pray for deliverance of anger, distrust, and unforgiveness. Your prayer, if accurate and specific, can begin this process of healing in someone's life.

In many cases, you are like the coach in a wrestling match with someone who has been a victim and is struggling to let go of the person and let go of the past. It is a life-defining moment for this person. Pray with conviction! Pray with authority! Try to bring the person to repeat a prayer of forgiveness. Speak what God is revealing to you at the moment of prayer. Throw that touchdown pass! Target the root, pray the word given to you by the Holy Spirit, and never second-guess yourself. God is in your prayer!

Application

Here is a prayer for someone seeking to be released from a root of unforgiveness:

Dear Father, there is pain here—so much pain that my sister is in desperate need right now. Remove the barriers in her heart and cause all extended grief, anger, and strife to flee. Release her from the grip of unforgiveness.

Now pray after me: From this moment forward, I humble myself under the love of God and destroy all attitudes of unforgiveness toward _____ (name of the person or the relationship, such as "my father") because of the hurt I have suffered. In the name of Jesus Christ, pour Your love over my past. I thank You that Jesus bore all of my pain and suffering on the cross. Heal all of the wounds that were inflicted by _____ upon me. Destroy my desire to retaliate, to bring justice, or to justify myself. I yield all my rights from this moment forward to judge and manipulate. Dear God, do as You please with those who have hurt me, love them as You will, care for them as You want, and clean my memory of any unforgiveness from this moment until I hear my name called into eternity. I pray this in the name of Jesus Christ who died for me. Amen.

7

Relational Need:
The Root of Bitterness

Knowing Scripture and hearing God go together. Revelation is 50 percent biblical and 50 percent spiritual. The Word activates the heart of God. Once you have discerned that the need is relational, unforgiveness is the first area you will consider. If unforgiveness in the life of an individual has not been dealt with, a root of unforgiveness can lead to a root of bitterness. The root of bitterness is resentment that has reached the core of human emotions. Bitterness leads the person to harbor hatred until it festers within and poisons the mind and very heart of the individual. Bitterness is a relational root born out of a refusal to forgive over a lifetime or even generations. Just as love is a decision and not an emotion, hatred is also a decision. In bitterness, one decides to hate, and to hold onto that hatred with an iron fist. Unforgiveness is the basic ingredient of bitterness; one leads toward the other in a progressive manner. When unforgiveness is ignored in a person, it tends to grow and develop into a root of bitterness. Thus, we could say that bitterness sits on unforgiveness.

Bitterness affects family ties, meaning that it is inherited as the children experience years of family history in which anger, fighting, and violence have been the standard response to life's pressures. This is the root of a dysfunctional family. You can say that bitterness is in the blood, moving through family lines and establishing strong and lasting roots in someone's life. When fathers and mothers attempt to solve problems with extreme measures, sons and daughters will tend to do the same. This kind of behavior is addressed frequently in the Old Testament. God abhors and repeatedly condemns the use of vengeance and hatred as an answer to human problems. In Deuteronomy 32:35 God speaks, "It is mine to avenge; I will repay" (NIV).

We find the Lord addressing the root of bitterness in Exodus 20:13: "You shall not murder." Murder is an extreme form of bitterness. Not everyone with a root of bitterness is going to commit murder, especially after they have an encounter with God. A root such as bitterness can be diluted because of the redemptive work of sanctification by the Holy Spirit. Even so, over the course of the individual's life, this same root will remain as the basic area of need.

First John 3:14–15 tells us, "We know that we have passed out of death into life, because we love the brethren. He who does not love abides in death. Everyone who hates his brother is a murderer; and you know that no murderer has eternal life abiding in him."

So you see that bitterness reaches far beyond unforgiveness. Bitterness is murderous hatred that lives within the heart of someone. It brings a spirit of death, instead of the abundant life that Jesus desires to give us. Obsessing over the memory of painful events from the past can cause bitterness. The root of bitterness perpetuates memories from the past so that they never leave or fade away. These memories may cause a lifetime of unresolved offense, which hurts relationships, cripples ministry, and destroys intimacy with God. The soul with a root of bitterness may react to loved ones with the anger and resentment of emotional hurts from years past, even though those events have no valid bearing on the present. The person looks at life with a cynical, negative lens, expecting the worst from life and from people.

Bitterness will affect the body more than any other root. One of the telling signs of the root of bitterness is the face of an individual. Bitterness can accelerate the aging process, making someone appear much older than she really is. The face becomes hardened and creased. The skin may look waxy or as though it is made of plastic. The degradation of relationships caused by bitterness can have a powerful effect upon the nervous system, the skin, and the general health of the individual. Diseases of all kinds as well as mental illness can be caused by harboring the poison of bitterness for many years.

When praying for someone consumed with bitterness, keep in mind that you require a miracle, because human beings can be very hard toward each other. Your prayer must be centered upon the revelation God gives you. Revelation can convict a person much faster than you can argue the case for forgiveness. Your prayer filled with revelation from God is your mightiest weapon in this war. You know that the need is relational. You know that forgiveness has not occurred and that the problem has progressed and deepened toward bitterness.

Do not begin your prayer in a distant galaxy, hoping to eventually get somewhere. At times, ask a question: "Can you tell me about your father's father?" I often begin there because the grandparent probably created the situation in the first place. The parents of the person you are praying for had mothers and fathers who were also victims of life. Asking this kind of question will enable the person to quickly identify where the hurt came from. If you can move to this point in your prayer, you have enough information coming from God and the person in front of you to really make a difference. Most people can identify bitterness in the family. When there has been a pattern of meanness, violence, and cruelty, these leave their mark on a person. Identify the poison of bitterness in your prayer and address it before going anywhere else. Pray toward the root!

At times, I ask the individual to take a deep breath and then exhale strongly. As he or she breathes out, I pray that anger, gall, and poison will be pulled from the depths of the person and released.

I received an invitation to preach in a Methodist church in a southern state. In the first service I noticed a man sitting on the last pew on the right side of the church. He was sitting on an aisle seat and I observed that he was extremely large, towering over everyone. Even when he sat down, he was taller than the average person. When the greeting time came, as the congregation began to shake hands and welcome the visitors, I went to this tall man and extended a welcome to him. Just touching his hands sparked a reaction in me. There was no doubt that he was deeply troubled and angry. His large shoulders seemed to carry a heavy weight, and he looked at me as if it was a matter of life or death. My sermon that day was from Matthew 18:21–35 on forgiveness. I could see the eyes of this tortured soul focused intently upon me during the entire service. When I extended an invitation to the congregation to come and receive prayer, I asked the local pastor to stay at the front and pray for those who came forward. I knew that I needed to go pray for that man in the back pew without delay!

I went to him and asked him to follow me to the first private room I could find close to the sanctuary. As it turned out, it was the men's restroom. As I began to pray for him there, I discerned a depth of bitterness and hatred like I have never seen before. I kept praying and the more I prayed, the louder his voice became, first crying and then yelling as he asked for the mercy of God. There is something unforgettable about a grown man crying like that—and this one was the biggest man I have ever seen in all my days of ministry.

Courage filled my heart, and I continued praying for him with a boldness that only came from the Spirit of God. I addressed unforgiveness and bitterness as the main area of need in his life. The Holy Spirit spoke the word *blood* to my spirit. When I spoke the word *blood*, something began to happen. He now started to yell even more loudly for God to help him. My time of prayer in the restroom for this hulk of a man lasted for more than two hours. It was like layers upon layers of hatred were being released from him, and I could not stop until he came to a place of peace.

Later, the pastor told me this impressive man was the master leader of a well-known illegal organization, and that he had come to the service desperate to be set free. Indeed, God delivered him of deep-seated prejudice, rage, and murderous hatred that night in the restroom of that church! It was not a pretty thing, and it took a long time, but our prayers were answered.

Are you willing to be used in the hands of God for someone in that much torment? If you are, then expect something like this to happen to you as you become open to praying for others.

Bitterness Quenches the Holy Spirit

Bitterness is directly associated with quenching the Holy Spirit of God. Ephesians 4:30–31 admonishes us, "Do not grieve the Holy Spirit of God, by whom you were sealed for the day of redemption. Let all bitterness and wrath and anger and clamor and slander be put away from you, along with all malice." The Holy Spirit will not abide where there is bitterness. Grieving the Holy Spirit results in Him withdrawing His anointing and power.

The fruit of the Holy Spirit and the gifts of the Holy Spirit reveal the glory of God through a believer. Bitterness, more than any other root, brings death to the fruit of the Holy Spirit. When people can see love, joy, peace, patience, kindness, goodness, gentleness, faithfulness, and self-control in the life of a believer, God is glorified, since mankind is incapable of bearing such fruit apart from God (see Galatians 5:22–23). However, bitterness robs a person of bearing this fruit, so that the glory of God is not revealed in his or her life. As the fruit of the Holy Spirit rots on the vine, the glory fades and the anointing leaves. Bitterness not only pollutes the soul, but it also consumes the anointing. The gifts of the Holy Spirit will not flow through the one who is poisoned with bitterness.

You will be amazed at the outcome when healing prayer in this area is well received. The person receiving prayer will want to bring all of the pain, hatred, and fighting to an end. Sometimes, depending on the situation, the Holy Spirit will have you give the person direction as to what to do when the prayer is over. There have been times when I have felt led of God to instruct the individual to approach the person who is the main object of bitterness and bring them a gift, perform an act of kindness, or ask forgiveness. I would say that in 80 percent of those cases in which the individual did what was asked of him or her, healing took place. What is interesting here is that some people refuse to make a move toward reconciliation, choosing instead to endure the turmoil and hold on to their rancor. The fruit of the Holy Spirit is paralyzed when someone chooses to remain in a state of bitterness.

Weighty, Crushed Spirit

"The human spirit can endure in sickness, but a crushed spirit who can bear?" (Prov. 18:14 NIV). A crushed spirit is a defeated spirit. The weight of so many problems and past hurts weigh heavily upon the individual, spiritually oppressing him. It is as though the offenses and traumas of forty years ago happened just yesterday. As you begin your prayer ministry, you will be amazed at the distortion in common reasoning and the utter confusion regarding the simplest things of life. It is here where you discover that when a human being has a crushed spirit, his or her outlook on life is sick. Don't forget that the weighty, crushed spirit is a condition caused by hatred and bitterness.

The root of bitterness replaces joy with mourning. This weighty, crushed spirit leads a person into helplessness and hopelessness as their default in life. When the past and the present are viewed as being bitter, the person holds little hope for a joyous future. In the Old Testament book of Exodus, the Israelites had known a bitter past in their four hundred years of bondage in Egypt, and they subsequently viewed their journey to the promised land as being bitter as well. Even though they had been miraculously freed from slavery, they still acted like slaves to the bondage of bitterness. They failed to see how God could move on their behalf in what they believed to be a hopeless situation.

Individuals with a root of bitterness see no way that anyone can help. They have no hope for recovering, and they frequently have no realization that recovery is even needed. Soon they begin to accept a state of helplessness and hopelessness as being the status quo. It is easier to be angry than to admit to bitterness.

How do you pray for someone in such a condition? First, remember at all times that it is relational. It has to do with others. You will have to identify the one who has profoundly and negatively affected this person's life. Do not deviate from this approach. The person receiving prayer may deny and even question your methods, but stay with the revelation! Never run away from a revelation. God is in charge of your prayer; you are not alone.

Control

In relation to the root of bitterness, control also has to do with feelings of helplessness and hopelessness. Power struggles arise and are won by being critical and controlling of others. Those who feel helpless and that life is overwhelming may try to control people and situations in order to feel safe and protect themselves. Bitterness causes a person to lose perspective in terms of others. In order to feel that one has control, a person begins to manipulate others for personal gain and become possessive of things and people. It is as though they made up their minds to exercise dominance in order to maintain power and never be vulnerable again.

For healing to come, individuals with a root of bitterness must discover those things that they want to control and why they are so compelled to control them. They must take a hard, honest look at themselves and their relationships with others and with God. To the person, she may believe that she cannot help being this way. To want to control others because of hatred and fear is a choice. It will be very difficult to let go. But she must come to a decision that she is sick and tired of living this way and wants some relief!

We fight bitterness by humbly allowing ourselves to become help-less before God, totally dependent upon Him like a little child, seeking His mercy and His help. When you pray for situations involving control, speak against all manipulation of others. Your prayer should address the problem with love and concern. Use all the gentleness you can bring. If someone is willing to receive your prayer, then speak to the need with authority and assertion. You must boldly pray against all kinds of relational attitudes, including control and manipulation, which hold the person in bitterness. You can speak directly to a human spirit. The Holy Spirit surrounds the spirit of man to comfort and console in times of need. Your prayer is able to hit the mark within the spirit of the person for whom you are praying.

No doubt, you are seeing by now that praying with accuracy requires boldness, courage, and absolute trust in the Lord. It is not a nice prayer that you come up with yourself to make someone feel better. God Himself gives you this kind of daring and effective prayer!

Destruction

A family can be torn apart by the destructive force of bitterness. One parent with a root of bitterness may express himself with such harshness, cruelty, and insensitivity that it changes the whole family dynamic. Destructive verbal or physical abuse separates family members one from the other. Walls of protection are put up and everyone scatters to find a place of safety. Because it involves family, children are caught in the web. They lose a positive sense of family identity and learn instead that hatred, revenge, and punishment are normal in family life. Sadly, they often go on to seek relationships where the same destructive behaviors recur because that is what they have become accustomed to.

I can never forget a visit to a church in the northern part of Georgia. The whole church was about to come apart because of bitterness. It seems quite silly, but the issue was that fifty years before, a member of one family had killed a cow belonging to another family. These two families attended the same church and during the revival both families came to the church for every evening service. As the first service began, I took note that the two families were in the sanctuary, but that they sat as far apart as they could on opposite sides of the church. During Holy Communion, each family was very careful to make sure that they did not come forward at the same time to receive the elements. I could not ignore such an obvious division. On Monday morning I went to the house of one of the elders, and he shared with me the history of these two families. It was public knowledge that they had hated each other for many years, and neither side was about to back down from the feud.

On Wednesday night, in our final worship service, I decided to invite the two oldest members—one from each family—to come forward. The two grandfathers came reluctantly. They faced each other in front of the Communion table, and I asked them point-blank if they were ready to break the curse of bitterness, which had destroyed the peace and joy within both families for many years. One of the gentlemen looked at me and said, "I believe it is about time." Amazingly, the other agreed. The Holy Spirit had been at work. A murmur of surprise came over the congregation.

I then read Hebrews 12:14–15 which says, "Pursue peace with all men, and the sanctification without which no one will see the Lord. See to it that no one comes short of the grace of God; that no *root of bitterness* springing up causes trouble, and by it many be defiled" (italics added). Next, I led the men in a prayer, which went something like this, "Heavenly Father, we confess that we have sinned against each other and against You. We ask forgiveness for all that we have done to our children and grandchildren, and we ask You to forgive us. Today we renew our commitment to walk in grace with You and with one another. Come Lord, and break the curse of bitterness that has hurt our families and our lives." At that point, everyone from both families came forward and a love feast took place. I later heard that there were more visitors on the following Sunday than on all other Sundays in the year combined.

Calling it out for what it was, a curse of bitterness, was enough for the Holy Spirit to bring conviction. The destruction wrought by the devil for years on end can be reversed by a single word uttered in the authority of the name of Jesus Christ.

Bitterness and the Body of Christ

Relationships are difficult for individuals with a root of bitterness because they fear vulnerability and intimacy. Bitterness can bring about behavior that is offensive to God and obnoxious to man. Prejudice and racism can often be found in those with a root of bitterness. There is a lot of talk about racism in our current culture, often without basis. However, the mind-set of racism and prejudice in one with a root of bitterness is real. A deep hatred and contempt for those of a different race, culture, or religion likely has been passed on through three or four generations. Differences in Christian theology can cause those who should be brothers in the Lord to treat one another with malice and scorn. There is probably more of this kind of bitterness within the body of Christ than in the world these days.

Many years ago I was called to preach in an old church in south Georgia. I arrived at the church early Saturday evening and I went directly inside the church to set up my equipment. As I went downstairs toward the fellowship hall, I heard thumping sounds and voices yelling. I peeked in through the partly closed door and realized that a fistfight was taking place in the fellowship hall of the church! I quickly went to the sanctuary to set up, hoping that no one had seen me downstairs.

I already knew what I would be preaching on during that revival: forgiveness! It was a difficult series of meetings. I eventually learned that the argument was over the chancel area of the sanctuary, which required major repairs due to the age of the church building. But a certain group of men in the church opposed the idea of construction and repairs, believing it would change the character of their old church building. I can still recall walking in the chancel area during the evening services and hearing the old floor groaning and crackling under my feet, as if it was about to give way. I invited the congregation to come forward for prayer, and the invitation was well received. Yet the group of men who objected to repairing the house of the Lord sat in the back of the sanctuary, arms crossed, completely uninvolved with the services. They held tightly to their grudge against the others. On Wednesday evening, the last night of the meetings, God directed me to a passage of Scripture from Leviticus 6:1–13.

In verse 2, God is speaking to Moses as follows: "When a person sins and acts unfaithfully against the LORD, and deceives his companion..." I commented that, although the matter in question was controversy and anger with one's neighbor, God looked upon it as a trespass done against Himself. This congregation needed to know what God thinks when we offend someone else. We frequently offend God.

I had preached four sermons and had not yet broken through, but this Scripture brought repentance to the whole congregation. Those men in the back hit the altar rail in tears and I was able, along with the pastor, to pray for all of them. We finished the service with the reading of Leviticus 6:13, which says: "Fire shall be kept burning continually on the altar; it is not to go out." Moses was referring to the fire of the burnt offerings that originally came from heaven. On the following Sunday, in the middle of the night, rain showers came with lightning. A fire started in the chancel area and burned the whole church completely to the ground! This congregation was given an opportunity not just to fix the chancel, but to build a whole new church building! Bitterness lost the battle here. Repentance had taken place.

Bitterness and resentment are most clearly not from God; even so, this problem is very present in our churches, especially among the leadership. There are pastors who have not spoken to one another for years over theological disagreements. Leaders are harassed by this plague of bitterness because they fear one another. In these cases, it seems that they cannot break with the order and be open to those leaders from the opposing side, because doing so might threaten one's status or financial security. We must deal with the issue of bitterness within the body of believers. Remember that the one for whom you are praying may have influence over many souls. Much is at stake when bitterness infiltrates the life of the church.

Condemnation

The misery that accompanies the root of bitterness can cause hatred to turn inward. The person may think continual thoughts of self-condemnation. John 16:7–11 tells us that the Holy Spirit comes to convict us in order to bless us and to bring us to wholeness. But, the unrest of bitterness makes it difficult to hear the voice of conviction from the Holy Spirit. The person in bitterness only hears the voice of condemnation.

What really happens is that you lose your self-worth. Since you cannot break free, you become a prisoner of your own thoughts. It is grievous to see brothers and sisters trying to live the Christian life, filled with bitterness and hate, suffering in every attempt to find fulfillment, and blaming others or the devil for all of their troubles! There is no real blessing, only agitation and tears throughout their miserable lives.

The soul affected by bitterness does not enjoy the mercy and grace of God, but lives in a state of guilt and condemnation. Romans 8:1 joyfully proclaims, "Therefore there is now no condemnation for those who are in Christ Jesus." To become free of bitterness, a person must know that the Lord does not condemn her for the past but is filled with love and grace to forgive and cleanse every sin. This is not because God is willing to simply overlook sin! It is only because of the atoning death of the Son of God on the cross of Calvary. Forgiveness is made freely available to us only because God sent His Only Son to bear the agony of sin and the curse in our place. Never forget this! Every single truth I am trying to communicate to you in this book is based on one thing: the cross of Jesus Christ.

I have seen many people, after years of pain and sickness, come to realize the level of deception within their hearts and take the bold step of forgiveness. They finally decided that they had enough and broke through! Are you one of these people? How long have you been in church, even as a spiritual leader, but have continued to hold a deep grudge against someone else? How long have you lived under the burden of condemnation, guilt, and hatred? Could the sunlight of God's love come to your soul and light up the place with joy?

I met a woman in Mississippi who harbored ill feelings toward someone. Let us say it right: she wanted to kill this person if she could. She was in bondage to drugs and alcohol. Her family was torn apart, with continual disputes and strife. After we met and I began to pray, I saw that she was finally at a place where she was ready to receive and extend forgiveness. Over forty-three years had passed and her mind, body, and pocketbook had paid the price for the hardness of her heart. I asked if we could go to the altar of the church. All I said was, "God, thank You for doing this." Her life was totally, completely changed. In the parking lot, she said to me, "I want you to meet the man I have hated for so many years." She took me to the church office. The man was the pastor of the church! I will never forget their reconciliation, their tears, and their hugging. God came into that office. I heard the report later that family ties were renewed. Her addictions to drugs and alcohol disappeared, as though a fresh wind of hope had blown into her life.

> The one who loves his brother abides in the Light and there is no cause for stumbling in him. But the one who hates his brother is in the darkness and walks in the darkness, and does not know where he is going because the darkness has blinded his eyes. (1 John 2:10–11)

An individual can be set free from the spirit of murder, the spirit of death, and the spirit of darkness. Simple faith against all odds will work! In the past, I have counseled for hours and finally given up. It is not up to me to bring healing to a situation that has robbed someone of thirty years of life. It is up to God to do this. Still, when a person is truly ready to be set free from murderous bitterness, confusion, and darkness, we all need to be willing to be an obedient mouthpiece for God. The Lord will use you, too, to do this. Simply speak forth with boldness, and let the Savior heal.

The Healing of Bitterness

Before his conversion, the apostle Paul breathed murderous threats against the followers of Jesus Christ. He participated in their arrests and executions. In 1 Timothy 1:12–14, he writes to the young minister Timothy:

> I thank Christ Jesus our Lord, who has strengthened me, because He considered me faithful, putting me into service, even though I was formerly a blasphemer and a persecutor and a violent aggressor. Yet I was shown mercy because I acted ignorantly in unbelief; and the grace of our Lord was more than abundant, with the faith and love which are found in Christ Jesus.

The healing of bitterness is nothing short of a powerful miracle. It is a miracle because the feelings of resentment have become lodged into someone's personality and have directed his or her attitudes and behavior. Christians and non-Christians alike suffer from bitterness and remain trapped in it, because nothing in their church experience has come close to addressing and healing this most agonizing condition.

When the apostle Paul traveled on the Damascus Road, he heard Jesus speak to him, saying, "'Saul, Saul, why do you persecute me?' 'Who are you, Lord?' Saul asked. 'I am Jesus, whom you are persecuting,' he replied. 'Now get up and go into the city, and you will be told what you must do'" (Acts 9:4–6 NIV). Notice that the revelation of Jesus to Paul was enough to transform his mind and heal him of bitterness. It all happened through a revelation!

Those trapped by bitterness need to experience the revelation of God's love and mercy in a close and personal manner. Their minds can be set free and healed in a split second when revelation comes to them. If you can believe in this powerful manner of healing, many things can happen to you as you pray for others. You must be open to the idea that God can heal such a condition. If you can be the conduit of God's mercy to a person infected with bitterness, your prayer can hit the mark and God can do the miracle.

Let us review the basics. Bitterness sits on unforgiveness, meaning that bitterness is a product of advanced or calcified unforgiveness that has not been dealt with for many years or even generations. Thinking this way may help you to distinguish between the two areas of unforgiveness and bitterness. Remember also that bitterness is compounded in its effect upon a person. Instead of only direct personal offenses, disagreements, and strife, bitterness is unforgiveness that has remained and turned into generalized acidity, poison, and gall within the personality of the individual. The person has become hardened and cynical. As the Holy Spirit leads you to the core need, inevitably there will be found a relationship that turned into vengeance, perhaps even spilled blood. It could be a father who was abusive in correcting his son. Instead of disciplining as a good father does, this father punished his son severely, to the degree that the punishment was far greater than the offense. In many cases, and this is almost a rule, there is blood in this person's past. If you reach back into the family history, you may find a grandfather who drew blood to solve conflict or an uncle who used extreme actions to correct behavior. It could have been an abortion that was forced upon a young woman. The need here must be found and addressed in prayer. The root of bitterness can be dealt with and the bondage broken.

Bitterness is a hurt that will not heal, a wound in the spirit. You cannot be shy in these situations. Accurate prayer has to reach the deep place of need. You cannot be timid and leave areas uncovered and untouched. I know that one of your desires in your prayer ministry is to know what to do or say when confronted with needs of this magnitude. Let me assure you that when you find bitterness, it will speak for itself. When I approach a serious problem, I am not preoccupied with what to say to the person; I am preoccupied with understanding what the Lord is going to do. Everything happens when you hear from the Holy Spirit and begin to pray. In these cases, where bitterness and poison is involved, it is God who must do a transforming miracle in the life of the person. When God begins to move regarding deep-seated bitterness, there is so much going on, all you have to do is ask Him to carry you along. The greater the problem, the greater the revelation!

Application

Here is a prayer for a soul trapped in bitterness:

Dear Lord, You know that the heart of this man must have a miracle today. Only a miracle will do it. The feelings and the memories are too strong and they bleed pain. Would You come and, in Your loving and gentle way, touch my brother with healing? There is so much hatred here, and there is bitterness that has made his soul sick and desperate for a touch from above. Please, intervene with Your love and the power of the cross. I sever all hopelessness. I speak closure to all incidents in this family that have led to hatred and perhaps even to the shedding of blood. Give Your son the ability to accept responsibility for his own choices, and to know that there is no condemnation for those who are in Christ Jesus. This soul chooses to love, to forgive, and to let go. We reprimand and call an end to the curse of bitterness and to what hatred has done in the lives of this family. By the most powerful name that is under heaven, Jesus Christ, I call forth today a miracle just as occurred in the life of the apostle Paul on the road to Damascus. Freedom and transformation in the name of Jesus Christ, the Savior! Amen.

8

The Ministry of Jesus

For so many years, I desired to pray for people, but when I started to pray, a vacuum seemed to form inside of me, diminishing my faith and leaving me with a feeling of emptiness. Maybe you feel the same way. Life's problems are so difficult, and when you meet hurting people, it often seems that all you can do is to hurt with them, since you do not have the power within you to change things. I understand. I have been there, feeling the pain of others without knowing how to pray.

I became tired of trying to make a difference, to really minister to the lives of others without seeing results. I knew that something had to happen in my mind and my being. Even though I was brought up in a minister's home and attended church regularly, the encounter with the Holy Spirit came much later in my ministry, after I became thoroughly weary of trying to do it on my own. I would discover, as George Müller wrote, "Faith does not operate in the realm of the possible. There is no glory for God in that which is humanly possible. Faith begins where man's power ends."[1] Prayer takes off when we stop relying on ourselves.

My father was a pastor and had ways of praying that were beyond my comprehension. From the time I was a small boy, I lived a public and highly visible life because my dad was so well-known. Even though my father was a powerful man in the Spirit, I remained spiritually nominal for many years. My mind and my pride kept me from learning and hearing from God. I have several degrees and a seminary education, but it eventually became evident to me that all my training was futile when it came to prayer. I have to say that my education was a blessing to me, because it left me unsatisfied. Thus, it moved me to hunger and to search for the deeper things of God. The time finally came for me to grow up and open my mind to what the Holy Spirit could show me in this journey. What happened after that only came to me because I felt so weak. I desperately desired to know how to transform my prayer life so that I could do something meaningful in terms of helping others. It turns out that feeling weak, inept, and humble is a good place to be. I had a powerful personal experience with the Lord of glory, and everything from that moment on was different.

I knew that my encounter with God was producing changes in me that would result in rejection by my peers, but by this time, I was too much in love with the Lord to ever turn back. I knew that I had to please God instead of pleasing man, but I didn't know how difficult that would turn out to be at times. Nevertheless, when one is wrecked by the compelling power and presence of God, what is one to do? The only way is to keep moving forward.

Consistent and Repetitive

One day I was reading in the Gospels and I noticed something amazing. I saw with completely new eyes how the Lord Jesus Himself ministered and prayed for people. As I compared the miracles and acts of ministry of Christ one to another, a methodology began to emerge that was consistent and repetitive. This revelation was revolutionary, and strangely enough, even frightening to me. I guess the fear was related to experimenting with an approach outside of the church norm, something that I had never delved into before. Yet I knew it was God who had brought this new insight to me in response to my petition for a better way to pray.

As I began to apply what I was observing in the ministry of Jesus, my approach to prayer gradually changed. A new clarity came to my mind about how to view every situation before me. The threat of rejection from my peers decreased as the years passed and I witnessed the undeniable results. Believe me when I say that your peers can be your worst enemies when it comes to spiritual growth. I also knew that most of these feelings were self-made and simply my perception of what others thought of me. Nevertheless, I decided in my heart that if I would purpose to hear and obey God, it would please Him. So I decided that I would fear God and not man. I decided that I wanted to hear God above all else and follow His Spirit. It was the best decision I have ever made in my life.

After meticulously studying every single account of the miracles, dialogues, and ministry of Jesus, I recognized that Christ was always sensitive and creative in the way He related to each individual. Every recorded act of ministry is unique. At the same time, I discovered a definitive pattern in His approach. Jesus employed a consistent and repetitive methodology throughout His entire ministry. For me, this observation was phenomenal. I was unsure of where this discovery was taking me, but the evidence that I was finding was very exciting. Was God saying that I could pray with pinpoint accuracy for others the same way that Jesus Christ did? Could I stop the guessing game of not knowing what to say when I prayed, or even worse, repeating what I had heard others say in their prayers?

The question became an obsession to me. How could I, a Brazilian young man, even come close to praying and ministering to people just like Jesus? After much study and prayer, I came to one all-important conclusion: only days after Pentecost, the disciples of Jesus began to pray for many all over the city of Jerusalem. They had observed our Lord in ministry for more than three years, and now the same Holy Spirit who worked through Him was working through them. They were employing the same methods and seeing the same results as the Savior! If the Holy Spirit so blessed them with discernment and wisdom to pray, why would He not do the same for me? Had I not been touched with the very same Holy Spirit who was present in the life of Jesus and His apostles? I was not looking to build some kind of big, famous ministry. I just wanted to receive what the disciples of Jesus received. After all, Jesus did promise in John 14:12, "Truly, truly, I say to you, he who believes in Me, the works that I do, he will do also; and greater works than these he will do, because I go to the Father."

Additionally, early in His ministry, Jesus explained to His disciples, "Truly, truly, I say to you, the Son can do nothing of Himself, unless it is something He sees the Father doing; for whatever the Father does, these things the Son also does in like manner," and "I can do nothing on My own initiative. As I hear, I judge; and My judgment is just, because I do not seek My own will, but the will of Him who sent Me" (John 5:19, 30). Jesus Himself claimed to be totally dependent and led by the Holy Spirit in all that He did during His three-and-a-half years of ministry on earth.

I began to study Gospel passages, one after the other, looking for a process I could apply in real life. First, I observed that the Holy Spirit brought Jesus directly into the environment where ministry would occur. Jesus did not wait for those in need to come to Him. He went to them, always being led by the Holy Spirit! This insight became key to my understanding. Ministry is created as you go. Seeing this opened my mind to a tremendous hope that the Holy Spirit would also lead me to people in need, one by one.

Seven Elements of Ministry

This idea of the Holy Spirit working through Jesus Christ in a consistent and repetitive way showed me that in any act of ministry, God is ahead of us, preparing the way. Jesus' encounter with the Samaritan woman, from the Gospel of John, is an excellent case study of the seven consistent and repetitive behaviors found in the ministry of our Lord.

Let us look at each of these seven movements. We are going to take our time, and I hope that by the time we are finished you can identify each element so seamlessly employed by the Son of God as He interacts with human need.

> So He came to a city of Samaria called Sychar, near the parcel of ground that Jacob gave to his son Joseph; and Jacob's well was there. So Jesus, being wearied from His journey, was sitting thus by the well. It was about the sixth hour. (John 4:5–6)

God had to be in this! John Wesley described "prevenient grace"[2] as the grace of God or the presence of God that goes before or precedes any movement of man toward God. The Holy Spirit was always ahead of Jesus, personally involved in what was about to take place. When Jesus came to Samaria, the land of Joseph and Jacob, and sat at Jacob's well, the Holy Spirit was deliberately and methodically leading Jesus to this encounter at the well.

Discernment

Jesus comes to a Samaritan city called Sychar, an area totally rejected by the Jews. Notice that environment plays a significant part here.

Jesus chooses to sit and rest at the well of Jacob. As He approaches, He is already working, observing, and measuring every aspect of the environment and the people who live in it. The environment is thick with rejection. At this point, discernment of spirits is operating in Jesus and revealing to Him the purpose for which He is there. This is a consistent behavior that repeats itself in every miracle or act of ministry in the Gospels. Even before Jesus spoke one word, a great deal had already taken place in this act of ministry.

This revelation was awesome to me because in my early days when I went to preach at a church and minister to people, I did not know that God was preceding me. My mind was always focused on myself and trying to plan what I thought I should do, not on what the Holy Spirit was already doing. When I received the revelation that God already had the plan and was way ahead of me in any prayer situation, what a blessing that was to me! If I would be available to hear, He would guide me as to what to say and what to do. The Lord would reveal Himself to me through discernment of spirits. This was tremendously freeing and like finding a treasure of great value. God was not only ahead of me, but He would show me exactly what I was to do and say. Breathtaking!

Note that discernment was the first act of the Holy Spirit moving ahead of Jesus Himself. If God is ahead of us in any activity that honors Him, then in this story about the woman at the well, this principle had to take place.

Confirmation

The next verse in this Scripture states: "There came a woman of Samaria to draw water" (John 4:7). So the next movement will be a dialogue or action confirming the Lord's purpose for this time of ministry. If discernment of spirits reveals something, then confirmation proves that what you are hearing and seeing is correct. When confirmation occurs, you already know that something wonderful is going to happen. As Jesus is sitting at the well, weary from the journey, a woman comes to draw water. Her appearance confirms that Jesus has indeed been led by the Spirit to this particular well. Her demeanor confirms that the Holy Spirit has brought Him here in order to minister to someone in great need. This is a consistent and repetitive element in the ministry of Jesus, found over and over again in the Gospels. I will never forget when I came to this discovery, looking through the Gospels, comparing Scripture with Scripture, and seeing the same progression happening everywhere. What a day that was for me!

Confirmation is critically important because it elevates awareness that you must be discerning of what is happening around you. You must be on the watch for confirmation. Where is the Holy Spirit leading you? What or who is He placing in front of you? You become engaged in the ministry of Jesus when you are observant of the moment and the environment around you. At times, I am more interested in what the surroundings are communicating to me or what the crowd is saying than in anything else. My family or colleagues might think I am zoned out, not paying attention to the matter at hand. The fact of the matter is that I am tuned in to the environment and what the Lord may be speaking to me at that moment.

For many years when I went somewhere to minister, my mind was fixed on what I wanted to do—my plan, my schedule, and my approach—not on what God wanted to do with me at the moment. I remember when I would automatically pray my regular prayer without observation, without hearing, without sensing the presence of God. Very little happened in those years of ministry. When my heart became attuned to what He was going to do, awareness of the presence of God tripled in my life. Once I directed my mind to a hearing mode, listening to the direction of the Holy Spirit, I could pay attention to what He was putting in front of me. You cannot hear God if your heart is thinking of what you are going to do, what you are going to say, and how you always go about your ministry. You must be listening as you go. *Prayer with accuracy begins with listening with accuracy.*

Let me give you an example of this. I was pulling out of my driveway into the street when I saw a woman in a car talking on her phone and crying. As I drove forward, I stopped my car so that my driver's window was side-by-side to her window. It occurred to me that perhaps I could say something to encourage her. She immediately opened the window, and I said, "Can I pray for you?" She readily agreed, so I began to pray. I could feel her pain and sadness. My prayer was directed toward her family (relational). I could see that she was married and that she was hurt and broken. The results of that interaction were powerful as she conversed with me, and I was able to invite her to come to our church. The following Sunday, her whole family showed up for worship. Healing had already begun. So my discovery was this: awareness. I became aware of the presence of God moving ahead of me at all times. I tried to be sensitive to what God was doing even when I had not yet spoken a word. At times, someone twenty feet away from me was already receiving my prayer, and I had not even talked with that person yet. This concept of awareness became valuable and powerful!

Again, I am reminded of the distinguished man of prayer, George Müller, who said, "I live in the spirit of prayer. I pray as I walk about, when I lie down and when I rise up. And the answers are always coming."[3] What a marvelous testimony from a man who walked in many miracles!

There are two crucial factors here. The first is that I saw the environment: a woman crying. The second factor is that when I approached her, she lowered the window. Thus, two things happened which are always present in the ministry of Jesus: discernment of need in the environment and then confirmation that the need is to be dealt with.

Jesus said to her, "Give Me a drink." For His disciples had gone away into the city to buy food. Therefore the Samaritan woman said to Him, "How is it that You, being a Jew, ask me for a drink since I am a Samaritan woman?" (For Jews have no dealings with Samaritans). (John 4:7–9)

Jesus asks the woman for water because the Holy Spirit prompts Him to do so. Confirmation that ministry should proceed can come in various ways. This verse actually shows Jesus providing an opportunity for ministry to happen. Jesus could have served Himself, but since the Holy Spirit had led Him here to interact with this woman, He asks her to give Him the water.

In my driveway story, I asked the woman in the car if I could pray for her. When confirmation comes that you are in the right place, all kinds of things can happen. At that moment, stopping my car and her rolling down her window activated ministry. The next obvious step was to offer to pray for her. Further confirmation came when she agreed to receive prayer.

Over the years, I have had many confirmations that the Lord wanted me to begin doing something or speaking to someone, and yet I missed those opportunities because of confusion or fear. Now my hearing is much better, and I try to not miss an opportunity to engage in Holy Spirit–led ministry. Many people cross my path. In the course of daily life, I pray for or give a word from God to at least thirty to forty people a week. *God sets up these appointments and confirms them.* My job is to pay attention to what He is doing and not to what I think. This is God's grace to me, and also to you. Pray that your eyes be opened to how God operates consistently and repetitively.

Jesus answered and said to her, "If you knew the gift of God, and who it is who says to you, 'Give Me a drink,' you would have asked Him, and He would have given you living water."

She said to Him, "Sir, You have nothing to draw with and the well is deep; where then do You get that living water? You are not greater than our father Jacob, are You, who gave us the well, and drank of it himself and his sons and his cattle?" Jesus answered and said to her, "Everyone who drinks of this water will thirst again; but whoever drinks of the water that I will give him shall never thirst; but the water that I will give him will become in him a well of water springing up to eternal life."

The woman said to Him, "Sir, give me this water, so I will not be thirsty nor come all the way here to draw." (John 4:10–15)

When you have an opportunity to pray for someone, what you say will create a response in the person's mind. What amazes me about these verses is the gentleness and kindness of the exchange between Jesus and the woman; how the conversation flows in the direction that the Holy Spirit wants it to go. It was as if the script for this interaction had already been written. In the beginning of my ministry, I spent a lot of time trying to persuade people with my own reasoning and arguments born out of my education and experience. I suppose I overstated the case at times, which resulted in little response and interest. These days, when I meet with people for ministry, I have learned to listen to what is being said to me by the Holy Spirit. I am convinced that when discernment and confirmation occur, your words will be exceptionally powerful. The conversation flows.

Root Work

Our goal when we engage in ministry to someone is to arrive as quickly as possible to the point of deepest need. When the Holy Spirit initiates ministry to a hurting person, there is an urgency in the heart of God.

This person has been suffering long enough! This is their moment! We began this chapter with discernment of spirits and then studied confirmation—which tells you that you are on the right track, hearing from God. Now we are going to move toward identifying the point of need, or as I like to call it, "root work."

Root work simply means addressing the deepest area of need. In the case of the Samaritan woman, the basic issue in her life is rejection of self. A vital moment in the exchange between Jesus and the Samaritan woman begins when discernment of spirits points Jesus toward her idea of herself. How did Jesus arrive at this conclusion? Discernment revealed a rejected Samaritan woman, used by men and abandoned by everyone. She goes to the well in the heat of the day, at noon, instead of the early morning hours when the other women go.

Why? It is because she is not welcome there. Her life has been characterized by acute rejection. The greatest longing of her soul is for someone to have regard for her and to understand her hurt and loneliness.

If you were the one there at that well in that same moment in history, the movement, the dress, and the demeanor of this woman would reveal the same root to you: rejection of self. When the root is identified, accurate ministry can immediately begin. The movement toward prayer can take place quickly since discernment leads to confirmation and confirmation leads to root work (the deepest need in someone's life). This pattern is consistent and repetitive in the ministry of our Lord Jesus Christ.

I have absolute conviction in my heart about this. If I begin prayer in the proper way—first with discernment, next confirmation, and then directly to the root of the problem, I will finish well. Never have I been disappointed with the results of prayer that begins well. As I began hearing God in this way, I no longer doubted the outcome of a prayer. What God begins, He will finish! Ministry began to change in my life, and fruits began to show up everywhere.

> He said to her, "Go, call your husband, and come here." The woman answered and said, "I have no husband." Jesus said to her, "You have correctly said, 'I have no husband'; for you have had five husbands, and the one whom you now have is not your husband; this you have said truly." (John 4:16–18)

Soul Ministry

In most encounters of ministry, you will dialogue with the person. In the ministry of Jesus Christ, the dialogue is always centered upon the core of the problem. A dialogue with Jesus is never superfluous, unnecessary, or shallow. It always targets the root and then moves to the very soul of the one who is hurting. At this point, we have advanced into soul ministry. This is the next step after root work.

The response of the Samaritan woman to Jesus is, "I have no husband." What a wonderful confession! Jesus already knows this fact. But it is an invitation for Jesus to deal with the deepest cry of her soul. All Jesus has to do is mention her husband and He arrives at the point of greatest anguish in her life. Isn't that powerful? A revelation that comes from hearing God is very dynamic! It is mighty! Soul ministry is a consistent and repetitive behavior in the ministry of Jesus Christ.

As the dialogue takes place, a miracle happens. It is plain that this is not a normal conversation. It came to Jesus by revelation of the Holy Spirit, and it will come to you in the same way if you practice the methodology used here. In just moments, the Holy Spirit can do what would, for most of us, take hours or even days of discussion. Does this sound impossible? Not really. When you become attuned to the ways of the Holy Spirit and His manner of breaking through layers of need, your accuracy will increase 100 percent. I could give many testimonies of people who have experienced radical breakthroughs in their prayer ministries by simply observing the approach found in the ministry of Jesus. Who can improve upon the ways of Jesus, our Lord and Savior? There is a lot to be said for doing ministry His way! Imagine how many hours of counseling you will save if you allow God to tell you what He wants to do for someone to whom you are ministering!

One night in Brazil, after a service that lasted more than four hours, a woman stopped the group on the way to the bus and insisted that I pray for her. I thought, *Do I have to pray for her now after being available for so many hours in the sanctuary?* (Yes, I know I told a story in chapter 3 that started the same way, but stick with me. This is a completely different story.) After a moment, I heard something from the Holy Spirit. It just came without me asking any questions of her. What I heard was, "She was too embarrassed." I knew it was God telling me that I had to stop and pray now. I felt the presence of God come over me and suddenly I had a genuine desire to pray for her. She knelt down, grabbed my hands, and placed them firmly on her head. It was confirmation to me that she believed in her heart that God was going to do something for her that night.

She looked to me and said, "I don't want to die. I want to live." I responded, "God wants you to live too. Be well." As I looked at her hands placed on top of mine, I saw rough skin and broken nails. She had obviously been exposed to years of labor and suffering. As I prayed, her hands pressed on me with all the strength she had. I found myself saying, "Spirit of infirmity, you have no right over this woman, and you are not welcome here. In the name of Jesus Christ, the Son of God, I reprimand you now." In my mind, I knew she was deeply rejected in life, without a husband and working hard to feed her children. I knew she had suffered with a deadly illness for some time, and she was at the end of her rope. It was now or never. I felt her pain, but I also felt her faith, pressing against my hands.

Three days later, she came to see me at another church with a piece of paper in her hands. Her blood tests had come back negative. Her HIV virus was gone! She had miraculously been declared clear of HIV. With tears in her eyes, she thanked me, and I, in turn, thanked God for such a marvelous experience! Later, I thought to myself how she did not come to the altar for prayer because she was embarrassed. But even at the last moment, the Holy Spirit moved through discernment to show me her need. Confirmation came as she knelt before God, and her soul cried out, "I do not want to die." All I had to do was to pronounce that she was healed.

When I first started learning how to pray for others, the concern that weighed on me was that in order to see results, I had to make something happen myself. I was worried that I did not have enough faith to bring forth a victorious outcome. I felt the pressure of people counting on me, and feared that I did not have it. However, I learned that I could not have been more wrong! Understanding how faith works becomes critically important if we want to move in ministry as Jesus did.

When my mother was diagnosed with Parkinson's disease, my heart sank to my feet. How could such an anointed woman, who had given her entire life to the cause of the gospel, be subjected to such terrible suffering? I prayed for her many times, but each time it was as though my spiritual battery was drained and needed recharging. As soon as the prayer was over, I would immediately feel tired and sad. A couple of years passed.

One day, I was at the mission in Brazil and was heading with the group to the hills of Santa Barbara, where the shacks of the poor cover the hillsides. I was in a hurry to catch up with the group, but I made a quick stop at the house of my mother. I placed a hand on her shoulder and uttered something like, "You horrible sickness! Why are you here? You are not welcome!" I said these words in passing and went on my way. From that day on, all of the symptoms of Parkinson's were completely gone from my mother's body. God had healed her instantly!

Now, please do not suggest that I did something wonderful, or that my faith had anything to do with that perfect miracle in my mother's life. She received healing instantly even though my prayer was so brief and without any real thought. How can this be? I have learned that what brings healing to people is not what you feel but what you do. When faith even as tiny as a mustard seed is put into action, it can move mountains. My faith was very small. What healed my mother was my obedience to the Holy Spirit regarding her need. What heals people is your obedience to move and to say whatever God is leading you to, so that He can do what He wants to do in that moment. Have you heard someone at the hospital praying this way, "God, if it is Your will, heal this woman"? This is a very double-minded prayer. Know that it is the will of God to heal. So just be obedient to ask for healing and kick the illness a little!

Command and Authority

When Jesus said to the woman at Samaria, "Go, call your husband and come here" (John 4:16), He was being obedient to the will of God. I call this movement command and authority. It is present in all the miracles of Jesus Christ, consistent and repetitive in His methodology. A command is a statement that exercises authority over a condition of affliction, illness, or bondage. In Matthew 8:3 Jesus says to the leper, "I am willing; be cleansed." This is a command. This same treatment is present when Jesus heals the servant of the centurion in Capernaum. "And Jesus said to the centurion, 'Go; it shall be done for you as you have believed.' And the servant was healed that very moment" (Matt. 8:13). When Jesus spoke the word, "Go," that was a command.

Following are other examples from the ministry of our Lord where the principle of command and authority is used:

And He said to them, "Go!" And they came out and went into the swine, and the whole herd rushed down the steep bank into the sea and perished in the waters." (Matt. 8:32)

"But so that you may know that the Son of Man has authority on earth to forgive sins"—then He said to the paralytic, "Get up, pick up your bed and go home.'" (Matt. 9:6)

But Jesus turning and seeing her said, "Daughter, take courage; your faith has made you well." (Matt. 9:22)

After looking around at them with anger, grieved at their hardness of heart, He said to the man, "Stretch out your hand." And he stretched it out, and his hand was restored. (Mark 3:5)

And He said to her, "Because of this answer go; the demon has gone out of your daughter." (Mark 7:29)

And Jesus said to him, "Go; your faith has made you well." Immediately he regained his sight and began following Him on the road. (Mark 10:52)

Continuing our study of the consistent and repetitive movements of Jesus in ministry, let's finish the story of the Samaritan woman:

The woman said to Him, "Sir, I perceive that You are a prophet. Our fathers worshiped in this mountain, and you people say that in Jerusalem is the place where men ought to worship." Jesus said to her, "Woman, believe Me, an hour is coming when neither in this mountain, nor in Jerusalem, will you worship the Father. You worship what you do not know; we worship what we know, for salvation is from the Jews. But an hour is coming, and now is, when the true worshipers will worship the Father in spirit and truth; for such people the Father seeks to be His worshipers. God is spirit, and those who worship Him must worship in spirit and truth." The woman said to Him, "I know that Messiah is coming (He who is called Christ); when that One comes, He will declare all things to us." Jesus said to her, "I who speak to you am He." (John 4:19–26)

I used to read the passage above as though it were a separate conversation and not part of the healing of this woman. However, more diligent study of all of the miracles and acts of ministry of Jesus proved to me that these movements of Jesus work together every time. With this in mind, I decided to pay even more attention to the end of the conversation than to the beginning. The totality of the miracle is found at the end of this dialogue. As the Samaritan woman perceives that Jesus is a prophet, and announces that she knows that the Messiah (He who is called Christ) is coming, a phenomenal statement comes from the mouth of Jesus: "I who speak to you am He."

Contact and Transmission

In the Gospels, every time Jesus Christ ministers to someone, there comes a moment when touching the person or speaking to the person takes place. It is as if the miracle is incomplete until some type of contact or expression transmits the healing and wholeness to the one in need. This action is called contact and transmission. It is here that the healing occurs! As you look at other miracles in the Gospels, you will find the Lord reaching out to the individual and making contact. In most cases He touches them, laying His hand on them, or lifting them up by the hand. We even find Him making mud from His spit and some dirt, and applying the mud to a blind man's eyes! Sometimes the contact and transmission is verbal, meaning He speaks the blessing. In this case study of the Samaritan woman, He brings the act of ministry to completion by reaching out to her with an earth-shaking truth that will change her perceptions forever. He transmits blessing to her life by revealing His true identity to her. She who had been rejected, cast off, and used and abused by men, is being entrusted by the Lord of the universe with the greatest truth any individual can know. She will never be the same.

Observe carefully the methods already employed in this one act of ministry: discernment, confirmation, root work, soul ministry, and command and authority have all taken place within a matter of minutes. One flows into the next. You can hardly tell when one leaves off and another begins. Now, at the final stage, contact and transmission is the impartation of a blessing to a woman in so much need.

The story of the Samaritan woman ends with the disciples of Jesus entering the scene, marveling that He has just held a meaningful discussion with a Samaritan woman of all people! The woman goes into the city to testify of this Man who has radically changed her entire life and future. The miracle is done. The Holy Spirit has worked through Jesus to completely transform someone's life. There remains only one more consistent and repetitive habit of Jesus, which is to look to the Holy Spirit to see where and how He should move next.

Check Around

Once an act of ministry is finished, God supplies direction as to what is to take place next. Without missing a step, Jesus moves as He is led by the Holy Spirit to continue His ministry among the people with grace and power. In some situations, He declares that His purpose there is finished, and He departs the region. At other times, He moves directly on to another person who is longing for a touch from Him.

Thus, the last phase in the methodology of Jesus is to look around and move in obedience to His Father. If God is leading you as you pray, you might as well ask Him if there is more to be done for others.

This initiative really blessed my life. I will never finish praying for someone without looking to see if there is someone else needing ministry. In a crowd of one hundred people, I always try to observe who is next, waiting for prayer. The idea here is that you do not want to be through if God has something else in mind. You want to follow and not lead.

Further Commentary

Let us review the seven principles of ministry found consistently in the ministry of Jesus.

Discernment

"Discernment of spirits" or "distinguishing of spirits" is a move of the Holy Spirit listed in nine gifts of the Holy Spirit in 1 Corinthians 12. "But to each one is given the manifestation of the Spirit for the common good. . . . the distinguishing of spirits . . ." (1 Cor. 12:7, 10).

We discussed the operation of discernment of spirits in chapter 1. I want to share with you two additional things about discernment. It is a fundamental truth that as you begin to pray with a desire to be on target, wanting to hear better for the benefit of others, discernment will begin to operate. As you train yourself to begin with discernment of spirits, it will become second nature every time you pray. All effective ministry begins with revelation from the Holy Spirit. So you must remain open to the idea that this gift will operate through you as you approach any opportunity for ministry. I made two choices: first, to desire that the Holy Spirit would move in discernment of spirits, and then to expect it. When that happened, my prayer life did not just change. It exploded forward with more faith!

Also, every person who has had a personal experience with Christ can have this expression of the Holy Spirit in the act of prayer. The essential point is to identify the One who is in charge here. R. A. Torrey puts it this way: "If we think of the Holy Spirit, as so many do, as merely a power or influence, our constant thought will be, 'How can I get more of the Holy Spirit?' But if we think of Him in the biblical way as a divine person, our thought will instead be, 'How can the Holy Spirit have more of me?'"[4] If you allow the Holy Spirit to be in charge and guide you in conducting prayer, you can be sure that discernment will operate. Discernment of spirits comes by faith and increases as faith grows.

Confirmation

Confirmation is looking for evidence that confirms that you are on the right track. You do not have to guess what is happening. Only follow the signposts. Never forget that you are being led by the Holy Spirit, so you must trust God with all your heart in this matter. Confirmation can come from Scripture brought to mind by the Holy Spirit. It most often comes directly from the one who is receiving prayer. It will not come from an outside source.

As I was praying for a man on one occasion, I wasn't sure that I was receiving any confirmation from him, or that I was hearing the voice of God accurately. I began looking all around as though more insight might come to me from somewhere else. But after a few moments, I saw that the man had his hands clasped tightly together and a deep grimace on his face. All of his body language was demonstrating desperation in his emotions and his heart. He was more than ready to receive something from the Lord. That was my confirmation. It can come through the eyes, the hands, a body movement, a sound, or a tone of voice. Always, God will let you know when you are on the right track and help you to continue. Do not give up! Give it time to work.

Root Work

Now you are about to get into the kitchen, right to the heart of what God wants to do. Always allow discernment to lead you into the target of prayer. This step will reveal the main need in someone's life. It is a critical point. Pause here with care; do not hurry. You could compare it to hunting. When you are hunting, you do not recklessly begin shooting your shotgun in every direction. You pause, you study the horizon, you check the wind, and you see where your target is located. You check to see that there are no objects in the way. It is the same with this area of prayer. You are carefully moving in on the primary need of a soul who desires a touch from God. Keep in mind that the person often does not perceive correctly their most serious area of need. This is powerful. The grace of God is at work, and your words in prayer at this point can tremendously affect the life and future of someone. I believe there is more wisdom at this point coming to you from God than in any other stage of your prayer. Things are coming into focus. Now you are seeing the core of the issue and you cannot miss it. Once you identify the root—rejection, rebellion, unforgiveness, or bitterness—you know where to go from there.

Soul Ministry

The mind, will, and emotions make up the soul, or the innermost self. After you have identified the basic need and spoken to it, the mind, will, and emotions of a person will speak to you. Think of what you heard from the Holy Spirit regarding the primary need in this person and keep guiding the conversation to that area. Due to the accuracy of the words you have already spoken in prayer, the person will often respond with conviction. They may look back across the years and try to make sense of things. These are precious moments where listening will really be necessary. Sometimes people who pray for others like to use a lot of words, thinking that the more words they pray, the better. However, when a person is responding to conviction, what you want to say is almost nothing! Let God do the work and you step back to listen! The listening here is crucial. If you interfere with conversation, you will distract the person from responding to what is being revealed, and you will derail the prayer. Think this way: what you are listening for is pain that is begging to be heard, guilt that must be dealt with, and agony that has been private for many years. Let it all come out and actively listen.

Command and Authority

When I was a small boy, my little mind churned constantly in my hurriedness to do everything and to run everywhere. No doubt, I was hyperactive in everything I did. One day I came home from yet another fight with the boys in the streets, my nose bleeding and my emotions stirred up. My father took me by the hand and sat me on his lap. He began to pray something like this, "Lord, this is my dear son. He is so much in a hurry that all he wants to do is to run and hit somebody. Now, in this moment, I speak to all his thoughts of impatience, agitation, and anger. Quiet him now!" I remember this prayer as though it happened yesterday. As soon as my dad prayed, it was like my mind immediately began to settle down. I was released from all of the fear and agitation. It was not too long after that that I was called into full-time Christian ministry while I was attending a soccer camp when I was twelve years old.

Command and authority is not something you do. It is something God does. All you require is to hear a word that will bring the problem into focus. Speak to that need without hesitation and trust God for good results. You have an entire company of angels, prophets, and men and women of God all standing behind you (see Hebrews 12:1, which states, "Therefore, since we have so great a cloud of witnesses surrounding us, let us also lay aside every encumbrance and the sin which so easily entangles us, and let us run with endurance the race that is set before us"). You are not alone. God is ahead of you. Do not be afraid. When you get to this stage, it is God who heals, delivers, blesses, and causes someone to be changed. It is not up to you; it is up to God.

Contact and Transmission

This part of our prayer is the easiest of all. The hard work has been done. The release you have been looking for comes from above. Always know that you are not the one bringing restoration and healing. You are a mouth speaking in faith, a conduit of God's power, and a transmitter of blessing from heaven to the one for whom you are praying. Learn to allow God to be exalted by recognizing and honoring His presence. What brings healing is His presence. You are merely agreeing with the Father for the life of this person. Contact and transmission can come by laying your hands on someone, taking their hand or hugging them, saying something that will bless them, or speaking a prophetic word.

Check Around

I remember the days when it took me an hour to listen to someone tell me all about their troubles. I would then pray based on what I had just heard. Today, fifteen to twenty minutes is all I need to conduct an entire prayer session from start to finish, and move on to the next person. What makes people want to receive prayer from you is your ability to hear, not from them, but from the Holy Spirit. When they are convicted that you can identify the elemental problem without a lot of talk, their faith is increased and they will be more receptive to prayer. In most of my weekend revival meetings, I set aside a couple of afternoons to pray for individuals who desire ministry. Dozens of men and women will make an appointment for fifteen-minute sessions. That is all it takes. In a matter of minutes, I usually arrive at the root of the need, and conviction comes to the one receiving prayer. After so many years of praying for others, I might miss the target from time to time. But eventually I tend to arrive at the point of deepest need. The fruits of this type of prayer are beyond compare! In His days of ministry, Jesus would minister to one, check around, and then move toward the next need. You can do this also!

Conclusion

Look into the Gospels and see that these seven movements are consistent and repetitive in all the miracles of our Lord. I came to the conclusions that I have shared with you by reading and rereading the miracles of Jesus and trying to comprehend the approach used by our Lord to meet the needs of people. I continued to be amazed that in every account, these same principles were used.

More importantly, I put aside every other ministry formula, and began to follow only the methodology of Jesus in my own prayer ministry. You see, the goal here is to minimize our own presence in the act of praying and to maximize the presence of God by hearing and acting upon His voice. This is the work of the Holy Spirit, not a specially anointed man or woman. As John the Baptist declared, "He must increase, but I must decrease" (John 3:30).

In the next chapter, we will cover several more case studies of the methodology of Jesus.

9

What "Consistent and Repetitive" Looks Like

Continuing our study with another example of a miracle performed by Jesus, I hope that it will become even clearer to you how these consistent and repetitive movements work together to produce a miracle. I want to overemphasize this portion of our study because being more attentive to the ways of our Savior as He walked this earth helps us to learn from Him. This time, let us look at the miracle recorded in Mark 10:46–52:

> Then they came to Jericho. And as He was leaving Jericho with His disciples and a large crowd, a blind beggar named Bartimaeus, the son of Timaeus, was sitting by the road. When he heard that it was Jesus the Nazarene, he began to cry out and say, "Jesus, Son of David, have mercy on me!" Many were sternly telling him to be quiet, but he kept crying out all the more, "Son of David, have mercy on me!" And Jesus stopped and said, "Call him here." So they called the blind man, saying to him, "Take courage, stand up! He is calling for

you." Throwing aside his cloak, he jumped up and came to Jesus. And answering him, Jesus said, "What do you want Me to do for you?" And the blind man said to Him, "Rabboni, I want to regain my sight!" And Jesus said to him, "Go; your faith has made you well." Immediately he regained his sight and began following Him on the road.

There are many recorded miracles of Jesus Christ within the four Gospels. The New International Version Study Bible divides the recorded miracles of Jesus into three categories: 1) healing miracles, 2) miracles showing power over nature, and 3) miracles of raising the dead. (A helpful chart showing all of the recorded miracles can be found in the NIV Study Bible, depending upon your edition, either before or within the first few chapters of John's Gospel.) This division helps us to better summarize and differentiate between the miracles. Of course, these represent only a very small fraction of all of the miracles and acts of ministry performed by the Son of Man during His three-and-one-half years of active ministry. According to the chart in the NIV Study Bible, twenty-three of the recorded miracles involve healing of the mind or body of human beings. Nine of the miracles deal with power over nature, such as calming a storm or multiplication of fish and loaves. Three involve the resurrection of the dead.

This example in Mark 10 clearly falls within the first category, as Bartimaeus was blind and in need of physical healing. (Other accounts of this miracle are also found in Matthew 20:29–34 and in Luke 18:35–43.) Let us look at this wonderful story as recorded in Mark, piece by piece.

Discernment

Then they came to Jericho. And as He was leaving Jericho with His disciples and a large crowd, a blind beggar named

Bartimaeus, the son of Timaeus, was sitting by the road. When he heard that it was Jesus the Nazarene, he began to cry out and say, "Jesus, Son of David, have mercy on me!" (Mark 10:46–47)

If you ever travel to Israel, I hope that you will have a chance to visit Jericho. In the sand dunes, rocks, and hills surrounding the city, you will find deep gorges throughout the Judean wilderness that are called *wadis*. In the midst of a dry, rugged, and desolate place, the wadis are channels cut out by the flow of water that comes during the rainy season in Israel. In ancient times, people used these wadis as paths or roads through the high rocks and rough terrain. Traveling from the new Jericho into the old Jericho through a wadi, which had become a busy road, Jesus encountered a blind man crying out loudly, "Jesus, Son of David, have mercy on me!"

We can almost smell it by now—ministry is about to take place. Whenever discernment is operating in the life of Jesus, it is because God wants to do something for someone. The gift of discernment of spirits is about to be activated for the purpose of helping and blessing someone in need. Notice that in the midst of the snorting and clamoring of camels and donkeys, as well as many voices being heard from the crowd and the disciples at that particular moment, it was the singular voice of this blind man that made Jesus stop. As discernment activates, the voice tells us a great deal. The voice is the signature of one's spirit. When Bartimaeus shouted to Jesus, his voice alone spoke volumes to Jesus. The text tells us that Bartimaeus "cried out." The voice exposed him as a broken, believing, poor, and submitted blind man. It did not mark him as someone who was proud, unbelieving, or argumentative. The voice revealed exactly who he was. Just the tone of the voice of Bartimaeus arrested the attention of our Lord. At this point in the miracle, you have the first consistent and repetitive element always found in the ministry of Jesus, which is the discernment of spirits.

Not too long ago, as I was preaching at a revival, a man yelled out to me from the crowd. I knew that he was a visitor from another church, attending the service that one night. It seemed strange that he would be calling to me in such a manner, but I began to make my way toward him through the crowded altar area. His eyes stayed with me, following my every move. When I finally reached him, he said to me in a weak and broken voice, "My Jena, my Jena, Brother Rick, my Jena." Just the intonation of his voice and one look at his face and his eyes were enough to break my heart. I heard his voice filled with fear and pain. Though there were perhaps two hundred people around us, it was as though I could hear his voice alone. It told me who this man was. The voice was not communicating pride, anger, or self, but rather fear of loss and despair. It was very personal and very emotional.

As I began to pray, his hands grasped mine. I felt his tears falling on my hands. I began to pray, "God, save Jena from death. Lord, this is not going to happen. Father, have mercy on this family." I prayed loudly and urgently. After the prayer, he told me that Jena was seriously ill and was in a coma following a car wreck. I have never heard from him again, but I know that God did something for Jena that night.

In your ministry of prayer, you will experience the presence of God when you adhere to these concepts because they are present in the ministry of our Lord Jesus Christ. Paying close attention to the components of environment around you is enough to open the door for an opportunity to minister. Discernment of spirits is not merely your observation of what is going on, but it is a revelation from God pointing directly toward a need. (A blind beggar crying out repeatedly for the mercy of God must have many deep needs beyond being blind.) As you observe who is around you, what they are saying, and how they are saying it, you will hear from the Lord what He wants to do in the situation. By desiring to hear and discern, you will develop prayer ministry that is impregnated with accuracy.

Confirmation

Many were sternly telling him to be quiet, but he kept crying out all the more, "Son of David, have mercy on me!" And Jesus stopped and said, "Call him here." So they called the blind man, saying to him, "Take courage, stand up! He is calling for you." Throwing aside his cloak, he jumped up and came to Jesus." (Mark 10:48–50)

When Bartimaeus hears the crowd going by, he asks what is happening. They tell him that Jesus of Nazareth iss passing by. After calling out, "Jesus, Son of David, have mercy on me," he is rebuked by the crowd, telling him to be quiet. But he will not be deterred. This is his chance! He only shouted louder, "Jesus, Son of David, have mercy on me!" Jesus hears the insistence in his voice. What this man is saying, and the passionate way in which he is saying it, reveals his desperate need.

Anyone who insists with God like this will get His attention. Jesus hears His followers rebuking the blind man, but He hears the blind man's voice even louder than the voices of those complaining. This is confirmation. Bartimaeus not only calls out once, but insists upon calling out again and again, and I believe the urgency grew in decibels. He will not be denied the opportunity to have his healing. Confirmation is present in every one of the miracles of Jesus Christ. In this case, the insistence of this humble man confirmed that ministry was in the heart of the Holy Spirit that day.

I have never been successful in prayer ministry unless a moment comes that confirms my purpose in being there, and directs me to the core area that God wants to address.

Discernment of spirits is the Spirit of God giving you information that you would otherwise not know. Discernment is meant to help you to move into the areas of most intimate human need. Some of us are in such a hurry that we do not listen to confirm the direction for prayer.

After years of asking God for direction and looking for confirmation, it has become second nature to me. Confirmation is a must in prayer.

Root Work

> And answering him, Jesus said, "What do you want Me to do for you?" And the blind man said to Him, "Rabboni, I want to regain my sight!" (Mark 10:51)

Here begins the next step in this miracle, or in any miracle of Jesus, which is to consider the deepest need of this person, that is, the root of the problem. The account of Bartimaeus notes that he is not within the city of Jericho, but rather begging outside of the city gate by the road. Other indications are that he had once been a learned man, yet here he is an outcast—not even able to secure a good place for begging within the city gate. The way the multitude sternly rebukes him reveals compounded rejection from his peers and society. The Lord Jesus, instead of ignoring or chastening him, takes notice of him and calls Bartimaeus to Himself. This invitation to come to Him goes directly to the core issue of this man: the root of rejection of self.

Jesus asks Bartimaeus what seems like a very obvious question to someone who is blind: "What do you want Me to do for you?" Why would Jesus ask such a question? It is because the response of Bartimaeus would expose his heart, who he really is. The root here is not that of a rebellious person or someone filled with unforgiveness. The root, confirmed by his voice and his humble spirit, is that of rejection of self. This is important, because being given this rare opportunity to express his desire to Jesus affirms Bartimaeus as a man. Likely, no one had ever asked this man what he wanted in his entire life! This question from the Lord Jesus conveys the love of God for him. Bartimaeus is a rejected man, blinded by years of exposure to dust and sunlight. When Jesus validates Bartimaeus by asking, "What do you want Me to do for you?" it communicates to Bartimaeus that he matters, he is cared for, he is not rejected by the Master! At that moment, healing must have flooded his inner being.

I am not saying that every poor person or every beggar has a root of rejection. However, in this case, the demeanor, the voice, and the state of poverty all agree together to expose the innermost need of the man called Bartimaeus. In my years of working with the poor in Brazil, I have met those who were proud, bitter, and angry. In the case of Bartimaeus, he is none of these. In his voice, Jesus hears a man filled with rejection but also filled with conviction and insistence to receive a touch from the Son of David.

What the gift of discernment of spirits reveals is just the beginning of what formulates accuracy in prayer. The next move is to look out for confirmation, encouraging you to continue, and then arriving at the most essential need of the person for whom you are praying. It is a moment of tremendous joy. The root is the basic area in someone's life, which holds the key to a miracle.

Soul Ministry

And the blind man said to Him, "Rabboni, I want to regain my sight!" (Mark 10:51)

We come to the next consistent and repetitive action, which is ministry to the soul. Once you have identified the root, you press on to address the soul of the individual by engaging in some type of dialogue. When you arrive at this point, you must be prepared to pause and give counsel or to hear a comment, which will help you to bring it home. You will recall in the story of John 4, soul ministry occurred when Jesus conversed with the woman at the well about her husband. Soul ministry in this story from Mark 10 is Jesus listening to the innermost heart of Bartimaeus as he says, "I want to regain my sight." This is his request. The crowd has been brought to silence. Jesus hears the soul of this man in his request and becomes completely connected with him as to his emotion and his need. This act reaches Bartimaeus deeply within.

After dealing with deep rejection in this blind man, Jesus now hears his fervent hope that he might be healed. A person's heart will speak out to you when you approach him with ministry that considers him to be understood, important, and valuable. It is a critical moment. It is a time to pause and converse a little with the individual. This is conversation directly connected to what has been shown to be the center of someone's most sensitive need. Thus, this conversation has direction, purpose, and meaning. It is not just talk; it is ministering to the hurting with the oil of gladness and the balm of good news. I use this moment in prayer to regain energy. Here is where I begin to ask God to come and move in the life of the person asking for prayer.

Command and Authority

And Jesus said to him, "Go; your faith has made you well." Immediately he regained his sight and began following Him on the road. (Mark 10:52)

The next stage in this miracle and in all the miracles of Jesus is the application of power from almighty God to the need. Notice that the Holy Spirit has been directing this conversation all along. It is like deductive reasoning, which brings many thoughts together into one final conclusion. It begins with Jesus stopping and hearing someone's heart. Now, He is at the focal point. As in every miracle of our Lord, another step needs to be expressed, which will make the way for the Holy Spirit to totally change the life of this blind man. The movement here is command and authority.

When Jesus issues a command in any situation, His authority is established. In this passage, it is presented directly and effectively in one word, "Go." Command does not have to consist of a lengthy dissertation. In Luke 8:48, Jesus issues a command to the woman healed from an issue of blood by saying, "Go in peace." To the man born blind, after putting mud on his eyes, Jesus says, "Go, wash in the Pool of Siloam" (John 9:7).

At this moment, what began in heaven now comes to earth in the form of a miracle. Long before Jesus came to the scene, God's heart was toward Bartimaeus. Jesus is simply following the leading of His Father by the Holy Spirit. This final act shows Jesus carrying through to the end what had already begun in the heart of God. Never forget, God is ahead of you in ministry.

How do you incorporate this movement of command and authority into your prayer? This moment, perhaps more than any other, will require of you! The need has been made clear and at this point in your prayer, it is up to you to complete the act of ministry with power. This requires boldness and courage on your part. But remember, the power comes from above. You do not generate the power yourself. God is the source of all power. Your only responsibility is to call it into being in the person before you.

Someone told me recently, "God does it all!" It is true; God does it, but He still chooses to use you to say one word, which will trigger the release of His power toward the need. In ministry, power is authority, but not your authority. You are merely a channel. All that we do in ministry is only by the power found in Jesus Christ. We are heirs, partakers of His power only because of His atoning death on the cross and His resurrection from the dead, defeating sin, death, and Satan. (These principles of power and authority will be discussed at much greater length in chapter 16 of this book.)

Healing begins with God. The revelation and power come from God, but the word that implements it comes from you! If you arrive at this place of command and authority, the probability of a miracle is very high. However, for this to happen, you must empty yourself of all pride, control, and fear. "The root of all virtue and grace, of all faith and acceptable worship, is that we know that we have nothing but what we receive, and bow in deepest humility to wait upon God for it."[1]

Having received God's leading, it is time to speak out the word that imparts healing into someone's life! It will be a command. Boldly speak what you feel is necessary to the prayer. One time I spoke with a loud voice to a man receiving prayer: "Forgive!" Likewise, it could be a phrase such as, "Let go!" or "Receive your healing!" or "So be it!" If you speak with a heart believing that God is with you it will go a long way in bringing faith into this prayer.

There is a Yiddish word that means "fortitude, fearlessness, and audacity." That word is *chutzpah*! If you are truly committed to see people healed, set free, and blessed through your accurate prayer, there are times when you are going to have to show some chutzpah!

Contact and Transmission

And Jesus said to him, "Go; your faith has made you well." Immediately he regained his sight and began following Him on the road. (Mark 10:52)

Contact and transmission follows command and authority. If authority releases the individual from what has been binding and holding him, contact and transmission brings the blessing that is needed. It is as though command and authority sets them free from the grip of the devil, and contact and transmission fills them up with the blessing of God! When you release a blessing through the ministry of prayer, you are releasing the benefits of heaven upon someone. It took me a long time to appreciate the fact that even though our Lord is powerful and can bless people Himself, He often uses people to complete His work. He used Abraham as an important person in the fulfillment of a promise. The same is true of Isaac, Jacob, David, and so many others. We are people who are chosen of God to bring His promises to fulfillment for the benefit of others. You have to believe that you can be used of God to bestow and impart a blessing.

Blessing is not something you hold on to; it has to be released. When we release the power of God through contact and transmission, we are reaching out to the person with the blessing of almighty God. If the word "Go" is a command to the individual, then saying, "Your faith has healed you" is reaching out to him—transmitting blessing. It is affirmative and it lifts up the individual. By saying, "Your faith has healed you," Jesus seems to minimize Himself in order to maximize the man or woman in front of Him. That is divine.

In contact and transmission, you have arrived at the last stage of prayer. Contact and transmission nearly always involves laying a hand or hands upon the person, or at least speaking a word that definitively calls the blessing to come forth. The consistent and repetitive behavior of contact and transmission is the culmination of what began in heaven and now releases blessing into the life of someone who has been longing for a touch from the Lord. This final act has to happen, and it will happen every time if it begins with God.

When Jesus says to the man, "Your faith has made you well" (Mark 10:52), this faith Jesus speaks about is once-in-a-lifetime faith. He is not referring here to the faith of Hebrews 11:1 but to the above-and-beyond faith that comes from God, spoken of in 1 Corinthians 12:9. It is a move of the Spirit of God within the spirit of a man or woman. This is a gift of faith from the Holy Spirit, a faith given from above with specific purpose and direction. When Jesus recognizes and verbalizes that God has given such faith to Bartimaeus, contact and transmission occurs. Bartimaeus receives a tremendous blessing upon his life, and he will never be the same.

Check Around

Immediately he regained his sight and began following Him
on the road. (Mark 10:52)

The result of this interaction outside of Jericho is a man restored
in spirit, soul, and body. Mark 10:52 indicates that as Jesus moves in
obedience to His Father, Bartimaeus becomes one who follows Him.
No longer classified as a rejected, blind beggar, he finds an entirely
new identity and purpose in life. The methodology found within the
ministry of Jesus produces grand results! Now Jesus, with His new
disciple Bartimaeus, moves on to the next appointment that the Holy
Spirit has prepared for Him.

Christ Jesus set an example for us as to how to do ministry, how
to pray with accuracy. This methodology of ministry repeated over
and over by our Lord in the Gospels is fascinating, and I hope that
it has encouraged you. I know that you want to follow Jesus in His
ministry, and to be used of Him to truly serve others, or you would not
be reading this book. God is true to His own Word. Just believe that
the Lord can and will use you to do the same miraculous acts as Jesus
did, and you will be amazed!

If you decide to take this seriously, it is possible that not everyone
is going to understand you at first as you seek to follow this consistent
and repetitive methodology demonstrated by our Good Shepherd, but
the blessings far outweigh anything negative. Know this: no one can
please God and man at the same time.

10

Ministry to Rejection of Self Case Study

By now one thing is very clear: Jesus always identifies and ministers to real need. He does not relate to symptoms, the clamoring of the crowds, or the prohibitions and traditions of the day. Religious leaders do not intimidate Him. His purpose is to reveal the heart of God regarding the real needs of people and to minister in the power of the Spirit. To observe Jesus Christ conducting ministry with accuracy is powerful and life changing. In his letter to the Corinthians, Paul wrote, "Be imitators of me, just as I also am of Christ" (1 Cor. 11:1).

We already noted that Jesus Himself says, "I can do nothing on My own initiative. . . . but the will of Him who sent Me" (John 5:30; see also 5:19). Jesus clearly states that He imitates or is fully led and empowered by the Father through the Holy Spirit. Consequently, the apostle Paul in essence declares, "I don't have my own ministry, my own model. I simply imitate Christ Jesus and do exactly as He did."

As you seek to minister and to be a blessing to others, who is your primary example? Whose model do you follow? This book is a straightforward effort to examine the manner in which our Lord related to people in need. Additionally, it is a heartfelt effort to equip you to apply the very same principles in your own ministry of prayer so that you can help others. You see, Jesus never misses the mark. He is always right on target with everyone He meets. It is my belief that you, too, can experience accuracy in prayer. The very same Holy Spirit who works through Jesus will work through you, and He has not changed His character, His ways, or His willingness to use a yielded vessel.

With this in mind, it would benefit us to continue a little more in our studies of the step-by-step methodology of Jesus. In this chapter we will look at how Jesus specifically related to those with a root of rejection.

Case Study One: Mark 5:21–24, 35–43

When Jesus had crossed over again in the boat to the other side, a large crowd gathered around Him; and so He stayed by the seashore. One of the synagogue officials named Jairus came up, and on seeing Him, fell at His feet, and implored Him earnestly, saying, "My little daughter is at the point of death; please come and lay Your hands on her, that she will get well and live." And He went off with him; and a large crowd was following Him and pressing in on Him. . . .

While He was still speaking, they came from the house of the synagogue official, saying, "Your daughter has died; why trouble the Teacher anymore?" But Jesus, overhearing what was being spoken, said to the synagogue official, "Do not be afraid any longer, only believe." And He allowed no one to accompany Him, except Peter and James and John the brother of James. They came to the house of the synagogue official; and He saw a commotion, and people loudly weeping and wailing.

And entering in, He said to them, "Why make a commotion and weep? The child has not died, but is asleep." They began laughing at Him. But putting them all out, He took along the child's father and mother and His own companions, and entered the room where the child was. Taking the child by the hand, He said to her, "Talitha kum!" (which translated means, "Little girl, I say to you, get up!") Immediately the girl rose and began to walk, for she was twelve years old. And immediately they were completely astounded. And He gave them strict orders that no one should know about this, and He said that something should be given her to eat.

Discernment

In any ministry situation, the operation of the gift of discernment of spirits is necessary because it is impregnated with information as to what should happen next. The expectant crowd in the town of Capernaum is not the object of the ministry about to take place. Nevertheless, observing the crowd is valuable because it reveals the level of the faith in the people, and the environment in general. In most cases in the Gospel miracles of Jesus, the crowd is always resisting faith. Observing the environment and who is present is essential, since these factors often bring contrast to what God is doing. The crowd is eagerly awaiting the return of Jesus, because they have certain expectations of Him. They have an agenda of their own. But Jesus crossed over to this area because He is led of the Holy Spirit to minister specifically to this family, the household of Jairus. It is imperative that before you begin to minister in any situation, you are able to identify where ministry should begin; in other words, where God is moving in the environment. God does not move according to the agendas of people. The Holy Spirit moves as He wills and where there is real need.

Discernment of spirits is the initiator of effective ministry. It guarantees that your beginning is correct and any movement forward will be guided and directed by the Holy Spirit. Why should ministry be based on human knowledge or input given by others? Why should we depend on the insistence or agenda of third parties when the Lord is the one to initiate an act of ministry? Jesus immediately discerns the spirit of Jairus by observing and hearing him. Jesus goes with Jairus by faith. He could have conducted a personal investigation of the situation, which most of us are prone to do, but instead He is obedient to the Holy Spirit and simply goes along to Jairus's house. He does this not because Jairus knelt before him and asked earnestly, but because He discerns faith and hope in this man. Because Jesus is attuned to the Holy Spirit, He is already ahead of Jairus!

An important thing to keep in mind is that discernment of spirits reveals the beginning of ministry and not the end of it. What you hear at the beginning is only a small part of what God wants to do. If you obey and follow the first prompting of the Holy Spirit, more will come to you as you continue with your prayer. You don't need to know how it's all going to turn out as you begin to move toward need. Remember this, God is the one doing the ministry. You are only helping!

Confirmation

Confirmation justifies and confirms discernment of spirits. When Jesus learns from Jairus that his daughter is sick and near death, He knows exactly what to do. Jesus has already discerned faith and hope in this man. Now, when Jairus speaks about his daughter, confirmation takes places. Confirmation is an essential element before you advance any further into ministry to the person. When discernment of spirits is confirmed in this way, it encourages you to pursue the direction that has been given by the Holy Spirit. It gives you confidence that you are indeed hearing from God and being led by Him. Confirmation takes place in many different ways. An emotional response, such as tears, might occur. The person receiving prayer might say something that reinforces what you have discerned. The Holy Spirit may bring a Scripture to your mind. Be on the lookout for confirmation.

Root Work

In each of these case studies, we are seeing that root work is of primary importance because it, more than anything else, determines the direction for ministry. What is the root of this synagogue official named Jairus? Pause right now and read the story again. Can you identify his root from the scriptural account? Is it spiritual or relational? Is it rejection, rebellion, unforgiveness, or bitterness?

Can you see the spiritual need in Jairus? Can you see that his problem is not relational? He is not proud, unable to relate, or bitter about life. He is humble and broken by the serious illness of his dear, beloved daughter.

Jairus says to Jesus, "My little daughter is at the point of death; please come and lay Your hands on her, that she will get well and live" (v. 23). Jairus is not only meek, but also contrite and filled with faith. He is asking Jesus to lay hands on his daughter. This indicates that he has heard of Jesus laying His hands on people and healing them. He hopes and prays that he might merit the same kindness and attention from the Lord as he has seen others receive. As they approach the home of Jairus, someone comes from his own house and treats him unkindly: "Your daughter has died; why trouble the Teacher anymore?" (v. 35). Here is a synagogue leader being corrected by his peers. When those inside the house laugh at Jesus and at the faith of Jairus, it is easy to see that Jairus is also rejected by his very family. Jairus has a spiritual need: a root of rejection of self.

If you are interested in accuracy in prayer, you must discern the root, or basic need, since it will lead you to the place within the soul where you must minister next. This discernment can take place at first glance of the person receiving prayer. When you see deep-seated rejection in someone's life, it is obvious. It is imperative for you to see how our Lord deals very differently with an individual who has a root of rebellion or a root of bitterness, versus how he deals with one with a root of rejection. Determining the root drastically sets the stage for how we are going to approach this individual, and what will be said and done in the time of ministry.

Now that we know that rejection of self is the root, we can proceed with confidence, understanding that the innermost need of this man is what he thinks of himself, how community sees him, and how God sees him. A major miracle is about to take place in his life that will make him another person. This is a good man with a big problem: what he thinks of himself. I have been telling you that this marvelous move of the Holy Spirit—discernment of spirits—carries immeasurable information. It is beautiful to see how it operates in this miracle of Jesus.

Soul Ministry

When we look at the flow of events in these miracles of Jesus, so much happens in mere seconds. One component of ministry flows into the next. "While He was still speaking, they came from the house of the synagogue official, saying, 'Your daughter has died; why trouble the Teacher anymore?' But Jesus, overhearing what was being spoken, said to the synagogue official, 'Do not be afraid any longer, only believe'" (vv. 35–36). Notice that Jesus overheard what was being said. However, He pays no attention to it, but instead He turns to speak to the heart of Jairus. These words from Jesus penetrate the depth of Jairus's being. Jesus speaks to the fear in Jairus, which had been propagated by the servants from his house. These words of Jesus have content and depth; they are designed to minister to the emotions of Jairus where fear has been unleashed. "Do not be afraid any longer, only believe." Soul ministry is a moment when discernment of spirits, confirmation, and root work all come together and are reinforced. Your engagement with the one in need is hitting the mark, and has now become very personal. You cannot stop here or leave the person unresolved. You have to see it through to the end, following the Holy Spirit in what He wants to do.

Command and Authority

Authority establishes the tonality of the conversation. Here, Jesus is not communicating in order to make friends or to preach the gospel. He is saying to those in the house: "Why make a commotion and weep? The child has not died, but is asleep" (v. 39). This statement is not only an affirmation of life but also a command. Command and authority is a consistent and repetitive behavior in the ministry of Jesus Christ. Jesus tells those in the house to stop crying and wailing, and He affirms that the little girl is already alive. She is not dead. Jesus rebukes the spirit of death and calls forth life. Command and authority has to be specifically and directly related to the need. In this miracle, Jesus shows us how it must be done.

Contact and Transmission

A miracle or any other act of ministry comes to a moment of transmission, or contact. You speak something in authority to someone, but you will be required by the Holy Spirit to move a step closer, that is, an action that releases the power of God to finish the job. Contact and transmission can be a verbal statement, laying on of hands, or a simple touch. In this instance, Jesus touches the girl and helps her to get up.

"Taking the child by the hand, He said to her, . . . "Little girl, I say to you, get up!" (v. 41). After Jesus speaks life into the child, He transmits power that heals her life. Though one may follow upon another, there is a great difference between speaking a word of authority and the act of releasing power. Power must be professed and confessed into someone's life. This is when faith acts in benefit of both the one praying and the one receiving the prayer. If you cannot say, "You are healed," then you cannot say it. But if you move in faith in this part of your prayer, God will honor you. I think this is the most difficult part of any prayer. Anyone can pray a thousand eloquent and heartfelt words, but very few will move in faith to push darkness away. I want you to move in faith! Do not be a weak person who is afraid to call healing and blessing upon someone.

Check Around

This movement is present in the ministry of Jesus on a continual basis. If you read the entire account of Mark 5:21–43, you will find that another miracle—the healing of the woman with an issue of blood—took place within the progression of events involving Jairus and his daughter. In many situations of praying for someone, you will be guided to continue to pray for another. When there is continuity in the process of prayer, it seems to spread throughout the congregation. Prayer that works seems to attract those with faith to receive it.

11

Ministry to Rejection of God Case Study

Case Study Two: Mark 9:14–29

When they came back to the disciples, they saw a large crowd around them, and some scribes arguing with them. Immediately, when the entire crowd saw Him, they were amazed and began running up to greet Him. And He asked them, "What are you discussing with them?" And one of the crowd answered Him, "Teacher, I brought You my son, possessed with a spirit which makes him mute; and whenever it seizes him, it slams him to the ground and he foams at the mouth, and grinds his teeth and stiffens out. I told Your disciples to cast it out, and they could not do it." And He answered them and said, "O unbelieving generation, how long shall I be with you? How long shall I put up with you? Bring him to Me!" They brought the boy to Him. When he saw Him, immediately the spirit threw him into a convulsion, and falling to the ground, he began rolling around and foaming at the mouth. And He asked his father, "How long has this been happening to him?" And he said, "From childhood. It has often thrown him both into the fire and into the water to destroy him. But if You can do anything, take pity on us and help us!" And Jesus said to him, "'If You can?' All things are possible to him who believes." Immediately the boy's father cried out and said, "I do believe; help my unbelief." When Jesus saw that a crowd was rapidly gathering, He rebuked the unclean spirit, saying to it, "You deaf and mute spirit, I command you, come out of him and do not enter him again." After crying out and throwing him into terrible convulsions, it came out; and the boy became so much like a corpse that most of them said, "He is dead!" But Jesus took him by the hand and raised him; and he got up. When He came into the house, His disciples began questioning Him privately, "Why could we not drive it out?" And He said to them, "This kind cannot come out by anything but prayer."

Discernment

As soon as Jesus arrives on the scene, He sees many people gathered and hears the crowd, the scribes, and the disciples all arguing with each other. Discernment of spirits is a revelation as to what kind of spirit is present: good or bad. It is not merely an observation of the incident at hand, but rather a revelation from God pointing toward the need that He wants to address. This is vitally important, because it is going to give you direction regarding your next move. Therefore, it must be a revelation from God.

As Jesus approaches, the environment is charged with disagreement, agitation, and unbelief. Anyone can identify anger, unrest, and argument. These behaviors are disruptive and confusing to anyone doing ministry. However, knowing that these emotions are in play is not enough to tell you the real cause of the disturbance, and what has to be targeted as the source of the unrest. Revelation given through discernment of spirits is always connected to someone in the crowd. Someone here is in desperate need. Effective ministry begins with discernment. If you keep this concept alive in your prayer ministry, God can use you. I tell you this once more with the fear of repeating myself too many times. How you begin a prayer is the secret to praying with accuracy. When you begin right, you end right. When you begin wrong, you end in the wrong place.

Confirmation

As mentioned before, confirmation must validate discernment. After our Lord questions those who are arguing, He hears a voice: "Teacher, I brought You my son, possessed with a spirit which makes him mute; and whenever it seizes him, it slams him to the ground and he foams at the mouth, and grinds his teeth and stiffens out. I told Your disciples to cast it out, and they could not do it" (vv. 17–18). Confirmation is powerful because it can actually correct the direction of your prayer. Perhaps you were ready to dive in to pray for the child, but as you hear the boy's father speak you gain clarity, and you know you must change direction. The biggest problem here is not with the boy, but with the father! Notice that the father, who speaks of his child, appears to be knowledgeable about spiritual matters (even more than the disciples), but he does not know how to deal properly with spiritual matters. He is quick to tell others what they should do, but he is unable to do it himself. Instead of being broken, desperate, and contrite, he is argumentative and critical of the others.

It doesn't take long for Jesus to identify that unbelief is the primary concern affecting the father. It is also present in the son, the scribes, and even the disciples of Jesus. When the father of the boy speaks from the crowd, this confirms Jesus' discernment of the entire situation. God reveals where the greatest need is and how to proceed.

Root Work

The father understands that a spiritual illness is present, but he lacks the power to deal with it. He brings the problem to the disciples, but they also are unable to help. Jesus Himself points toward the root or basic need in this way: "And He answered them and said, 'O unbelieving generation, how long shall I be with you? How long shall I put up with you?'" (v. 19). He is speaking in broad strokes to the scribes, the disciples, the father, and the boy. Because rebellion is characterized by unbelief—the exalting of argument, thought, and reason above the intimate knowledge of God—rebellion is the root in this case. The father seems to comprehend that there is an evil influence upon his son. But his knowledge is not based upon discernment of spirits. It is based upon his personal experience of rebelliously seeking other gods in order to find answers. *Rebellion* is a grim word to describe the father's need, but that is exactly what we are dealing with here. A mind that worships itself, rationalization that questions faith and speaks doubt, and a theological behavior that exalts itself above the Holy Spirit is nothing but rebellion against God. This father is the type of Christian who knows a lot about religion and spiritual practices, but who is utterly devoid of humility and faith.

Soul Ministry

In this account found in Mark 9:14–29, we see Jesus at the height of sensitivity and wisdom as He ministers to the soul of this father. To my mind, it is second in this respect only to Jesus' encounter with the Samaritan woman in John 4.

> And He asked his father, "How long has this been happening to him?" And he said, "From childhood. It has often thrown him both into the fire and into the water to destroy him. But if You can do anything, take pity on us and help us!" And Jesus said to him, "'If You can?' All things are possible to him who believes." Immediately the boy's father cried out and said, "I do believe; help my unbelief." (Mark 9:21–24)

When Jesus asks how long the infirmity has existed, the response of the father exposes him as one who has had vast experience with spiritual phenomenon, but lacks the faith and the power to do anything about it. He is strong in personality, theology, and opinions, but he is bankrupt when it comes to faith. This is the heart of the matter. From here on, ministry to his soul takes place. Which area of his soul receives the most ministry? Rebellion is a matter of the mind. The father is finally convicted in the presence of Jesus that his self-sufficiency has gotten him nowhere and that he desperately needs faith. Under conviction for his lack of faith, the father cries out to receive the faith of a child. Jesus confronts his unbelieving heart in an accurate and powerful act of ministry. Soul ministry has taken place.

Command and Authority

There is no doubt that there is an evil spirit in the boy. That fact has never been in question. However, the great revelation is that it is the father who has been holding things back. Since the father has now been convicted of his lack of faith, the son may receive the ministry he needs. Authority identifies the need by name, and accurate prayer at this stage will bring results. Jesus pronounces words of command: "He rebuked the unclean spirit, saying to it, 'You deaf and mute spirit, I command you, come out of him and do not enter him again.' After crying out and throwing him into terrible convulsions, it came out; and the boy became so much like a corpse that most of them said, 'He is dead!'" (vv. 25–26).

When you are confronting evil, you must speak the words of command and authority with decisiveness. I have never seen anyone blessed in these situations if the one offering the prayer shrinks back in timidity at this moment or tries to be nice. You are dealing with evil. It is something from the pit of hell holding another in terrible bondage. If you must command, then command! Say it with authority and courage. If you want to move in accurate, powerful prayer, this is not the time to please others.

Contact and Transmission

The transmission is direct and to the point. We may easily pass over the movement of Jesus helping someone stand to his feet, but it is very relevant. Jesus would not walk away without fulfilling the entire purpose of ministry to the boy. "But Jesus took him by the hand and raised him; and he got up" (v. 27).

The action of taking the boy by the hand and helping him up is a classic move by Jesus. It communicates love and validation to this young man who has suffered so much. It verifies that he has been released to live the life of a normal child. Even without words, the touch itself meets a deep need in the boy to be treated with dignity and tenderness. In that moment, the power of God makes contact with the boy and literally raises him up to have hope for a completely different future from here on. The ministry of Jesus in contact and transmission can be a word, a touch, and sometimes both. If you have arrived to this point in prayer, you have accomplished something wondrous.

Check Around

"When He came into the house, His disciples began questioning Him privately, 'Why could we not drive it out?' And He said to them, 'This kind cannot come out by anything but prayer" (vv. 28–29).

Following the leading of the Holy Spirit, Jesus moves to the next need—that of the disciples. Their inability to cast out the demon causes them to have a crisis of faith. Jesus helps them by taking time to talk with them in private. He explains the importance of a lifestyle of fasting and prayer if they are ever going to be able to effectively minister in chaotic circumstances such as this. Ministry that is led of God will continue until the whole need is completely dealt with. Nothing is over until God says so. This might be disruptive to the normal bedside manner of any preacher or lay person doing prayer ministry. We have our methodologies that we like to follow, but if you want to have success in prayer, learn this principle: nothing is over until the Holy Spirit is finished doing whatever He is doing. Since the disciples themselves are unable to deal with the need, our Lord has to turn to them immediately and explain what they are lacking. He uses this event as a teaching and equipping moment in the lives of the disciples.

As you pray for people, try not to remove yourself from the scene too quickly by leaving in a hurry. Listen to the inner voice of the Holy Spirit and ask Him if there is anything else He wants you to address. This will bless you abundantly.

12

Ministry to Unforgiveness Case Study

Case Study Three: Mark 2:1–13

When He had come back to Capernaum several days afterward, it was heard that He was at home. And many were gathered together, so that there was no longer room, not even near the door; and He was speaking the word to them. And they came, bringing to Him a paralytic, carried by four men. Being unable to get to Him because of the crowd, they removed the roof above Him; and when they had dug an opening, they let down the pallet on which the paralytic was lying. And Jesus seeing their faith said to the paralytic, "Son, your sins are forgiven." But some of the scribes were sitting there and reasoning in their hearts, "Why does this man speak that way? He is blaspheming; who can forgive sins but God alone?" Immediately Jesus, aware in His spirit that they were reasoning that way within themselves, said to them, "Why are you reasoning about these things in your hearts? Which is easier, to say to the paralytic, "Your sins are forgiven"; or to say, "Get up, and pick up your pallet and walk"? But so that you may know that the Son of Man has authority on earth to forgive sins"—He said to the paralytic, "I say to you, get up, pick up your pallet and go home." And he got up and immediately picked up the pallet and went out in the sight of everyone, so that they were all amazed and were glorifying God, saying, "We have never seen anything like this."

And He went out again by the seashore; and all the people were coming to Him, and He was teaching them.

Discernment

Jesus Christ our Lord is conscious of the environment of unbelief in Capernaum. His hometown was Nazareth, but He came here in fulfillment of what was said through the prophet Isaiah:

> Now when Jesus heard that John had been taken into custody, He withdrew into Galilee; and leaving Nazareth, He came to settle in Capernaum, which is by the sea, in the region of Zebulon and Naphtali. This was to fulfill what was spoken through Isaiah the prophet, saying, "The Land of Zebulun and the Land of Naphtali, by the way of the sea, beyond the Jordan, Galilee of the Gentiles—The people who were sitting in darkness saw a great light, and those who were sitting in the land and shadow of death, upon them a light dawned." From that time Jesus began to preach and say, "Repent, for the kingdom of heaven is at hand." (Matt. 4:12–17)

As word spreads that Jesus has made His home in Capernaum, so many gather to hear Him that the house is literally enveloped in people.

When Jesus sees that four men have made a hole in the roof in order to gain access into His presence, He discerns outstanding faith in them. The scripture in Mark 2 says, "Seeing their faith..." (v. 5). Discernment of spirits is looking for the substance of the need. Obviously this man had real friends who cared for him in his sad condition. No one would go to such lengths as to make a hole in the roof without amazing faith and unstoppable commitment. Rebellion is not the problem here, for where there is genuine faith, there is no rebellion. If your discernment is focused upon the crowd, you would arrive at the wrong conclusion. In the crowd there is plenty of rebellion, but in the heart of the paralytic there is faith and hope because of his friends.

Thus, you have to pay close attention to how Jesus immediately discerns uncompromising faith in the four men who brought the paralytic to Him. There are many that day seeking healing, but here is one who is surrounded by energetic, positive faith. This means that the problem with the man is more of a relational nature, not spiritual. Relational need is directly connected with others. This man is truly loved, but in his heart he still holds unforgiveness toward others and most assuredly against himself. He needs to know that his sin is forgiven before he can be free.

Confirmation

The four men taking such drastic measures as lowering a man through a hole in a roof, even as Jesus is speaking, confirms that these men acted in faith. When Jesus, prompted by the Holy Spirit, says to the man, "Son, your sins are forgiven" (v. 5), this confirms the heart of the matter. This illness is directly related to sin involving a relational issue with others. Perhaps the man had been deeply hurt, and would not let the pain and the blame go. The sin of unforgiveness is holding him in a place of torture to the point that his body is paralyzed.

Root Work

It is not unusual for an individual with a root of unforgiveness to suffer with physical sicknesses. The key to this man's physical healing is not a physical touch—it is forgiveness. Once the man knows that his sins are forgiven, he can receive healing for the paralysis. As the root is identified, Jesus, without hesitation, addresses unforgiveness in the paralyzed man. The core of the problem is not physical; it is a relational need. Praying with accuracy arrives at the point of need in a matter of seconds.

Now would be a good time for me to share something of great value with you, if you are hoping to pray with accuracy for sick people and see results. Not all disease and infirmity has the same fundamental cause. In other words, not all illness is just an illness. To pray with accuracy for someone who needs healing, you first must discern the reason for the illness. In the whole of the Old Testament and New Testament, and especially in the recorded ministry of Jesus in the four Gospels, we can see that Scripture identifies five causes of illness. These five are: 1) sin, 2) sins of others, 3) hereditary, 4) demonic, or 5) for the glory of God.

What this tells us is that if someone is ill because of sin that has not been dealt with, all the prayer in the world for simple physical healing will yield very little results. Therefore, you must seek revelation from God regarding the source (the genesis of the infirmity) if you are to begin your prayer in the right place.

This is the only place in the miracles of Jesus where the root is verbally spoken by the Master: "Son, your sins are forgiven." Jesus knows without a doubt that the sin of unforgiveness is the culprit that has kept him in his agonizing state. The question that begs an answer is this: Can carrying unforgiveness toward someone actually make you sick? Let us see what our Lord teaches about this in one of His parables:

> "For this reason the kingdom of heaven may be compared to a
> king who wished to settle accounts with his slaves. And when

he had begun to settle them, one who owed him ten thousand talents was brought to him. But since he did not have the means to repay, his lord commanded him to be sold, along with his wife and children and all that he had, and repayment to be made. So the slave fell to the ground and prostrated himself before him, saying, 'Have patience with me and I will repay you everything.' And the lord of that slave felt compassion and released him and forgave him the debt. But that slave went out and found one of his fellow slaves who owed him a hundred denarii; and he seized him and began to choke him, saying, 'Pay back what you owe.' So his fellow slave fell down and began to plead with him, saying, 'Have patience with me and I will repay you.' But he was unwilling and went out and threw him in prison until he should pay back what was owed. So when his fellow slaves saw what had happened, they were deeply grieved and came and reported to their lord all that had happened. Then summoning him, his lord said to him, 'You wicked slave, I forgave you all that debt because you pleaded with me. Should you not also have had mercy on your fellow slave, in the same way that I had mercy on you?' And his lord, moved with anger, handed him over to the torturers until he should repay all that was owed him. My Heavenly Father will also do the same to you, if each of you does not forgive his brother from your heart." (Matt. 18:23–35)

Yes, unforgiveness can keep a person in a place of mental, emotional, and physical torture. The root to be addressed here is unforgiveness. Stick to the root and speak to it with authority and boldness. Remember that graciousness is the best way. Speak kindly, speak clearly, never doubting, and without second-guessing what you say. Speak with faith and let it take its course. Praying the Word will always bless those receiving the prayer.

Soul Ministry

The identification of unforgiveness as a root or basic need in the individual will lead to the area of the soul that must be targeted. When accurate prayer penetrates the very soul, conviction often touches the emotions powerfully. At this juncture, you have arrived at the key area, and it becomes very up close and personal. In this case, Jesus says to the man, "Son, your sins are forgiven" (v. 5). The title "son" ministers to this man more than anything else said or done in the passage. This is an act of love and kindness, which reaches deep into the paralytic's broken and hurting emotions. The intent of Jesus is to meet the greatest need, which is for him to know forgiveness. The man's response to forgiveness is the ability to receive healing for his bodily disease. Because the Jewish mind-set of the day was that all sickness is caused by sin, an indictment of guilt and shame is placed upon anyone who had an infirmity. The general mind-set is that if someone is sick, he or she must have done something to deserve such suffering. Therefore, this extension of grace spoken in the presence of everyone by the Master is amazing, relieving the man of his heavy burden of condemnation, and removing an enormous weight off of his soul. Jesus continues to minister wholeness to the man's soul by sending him home to rejoice with his family and to show them what has happened to him.

Command and Authority

The act of ministry will not be finalized if these last two stages are not implemented. Note that Jesus commands both forgiveness and healing: "Son, your sins are forgiven" (v. 5) and "Get up, pick up your pallet and go home" (v. 11). The main command here is: "Get up."

For one who has been totally paralyzed, this word carries dynamic power. Never forget, when implementing authority in an act of ministry, the power does not come from you. However, you must release it into the situation before you. For this to happen, you have to speak it out. Because of our lack of faith or inability to accept certain spiritual principles, we often succumb to unbelief. At times our demeanor is weak because we are overly concerned about our reputation, our place of respect, or our theology coming into question.

How can you overcome this fear-based behavior? One suggestion is that you do what is the most uncomfortable thing you have ever done! If you ask those who have been around me for a while, they can tell you stories of times when my behavior or bedside manner was somewhat questionable! I had to overdo it in order to overcome my feeling of having nothing to give. When I finally arrived to the place where I honestly did not care what others would think of me, God began to do marvelous things. The Lord was gracious and gave me much fruit because of my faith and outright audacity. But it took a while, because my lack of faith had been blocking the power of God. Do not let this happen to you. Think of those four men who were so determined to obtain a blessing for their friend that they tore the roof apart right over Jesus' head as He taught. What was the Lord's response to such chutzpah? He loved it!

Contact and Transmission

First, Jesus validates the working of this miracle when He publicly rebukes the scribes for their rebellious and unbelieving thoughts:

> Immediately Jesus, aware in His spirit that they were reasoning that way within themselves, said to them, "Why are you reasoning about these things in your hearts? Which is easier, to say to the paralytic, 'Your sins are forgiven'; or to say, 'Get up, and pick up your pallet and walk'? But so that that you may know that the Son of Man has authority on earth to forgive sins ..." (vv. 8–10a)

Next in this act of ministry in Mark 2, contact and transmission is done through a simple phrase spoken to the paralytic: "He said to the paralytic, 'I say to you, get up, pick up your pallet and go home.' And he got up and immediately picked up the pallet and went out in the sight of everyone, so that they were all amazed and were glorifying God, saying, 'We have never seen anything like this'" (vv. 10b–12).

Transmitting means that you are now passing to the receiving party what has already been done by the Holy Spirit. You are not creating anything or working anything up emotionally. You are only connecting the dots here. When Jesus Christ releases power to heal, it starts with the man arising or standing up. Anyone standing up after being paralyzed is already a miracle! But something more had to be said in order for the miracle to be cemented in his mind, so that he would not doubt or crumble. Our Lord said this: "Pick up your pallet and go home."

In other words, an action of faith must be performed in order to complete the healing. During contact and transmission, Jesus requires the paralytic to move by actively doing two things: picking up his pallet and heading home. There is something vitally important about someone who has lain helpless for years being able to demonstrate that he can now move and act as a healthy, whole human being. The scripture says he "went out in the sight everyone" (v. 12). The ability of the man to pick up his pallet and walk "in the sight of everyone" testifies that the bondage of guilt, shame, and unforgiveness has been lifted from him and he is now a free man.

Check Around

Following the healing episode, Jesus departs the house and walks down to the seashore, where He teaches the Word of God to the crowd who follows Him: "And He went out again by the seashore; and all the people were coming to Him, and He was teaching them" (v. 13). The shore of the Sea of Galilee lies just a few meters from the city limits of Capernaum. The multitude, which had surrounded the house, is still hungry to hear what Jesus has to say. The Lord moves to a location close by and takes up where He had left off when He was interrupted by the men on the roof.

After prayer ministry is over and God has done a beautiful healing, be available and ready for what the Lord wants to do next. Be aware of the continuity of ministry. God might have something else for you to do. Just slowing down and hearing from Him will bless you beyond measure.

13

Ministry to Bitterness Case Study

Case Study Four: Mark 5:1–20

They came to the other side of the sea, into the country of the Gerasenes [Some translations say "Gadarenes."] When He got out of the boat, immediately a man from the tombs with an unclean spirit met Him, and he had his dwelling among the tombs. And no one was able to bind him anymore, even with a chain; because he had often been bound with shackles and chains, and the chains had been torn apart by him and the shackles broken in pieces, and no one was strong enough to subdue him. Constantly, night and day, he was screaming among the tombs and in the mountains, and gashing himself with stones. Seeing Jesus from a distance, he ran up and bowed down before Him; and shouting with a loud voice, he said, "What business do we have with each other, Jesus, Son of the Most High God? I implore You by God, do not torment me!" For He had been saying to him, "Come out of the man, you unclean spirit!" And He was asking him, "What is your name?" And he said to Him, "My name is Legion; for we are many." And he began to implore Him earnestly not to send them out of the country. Now there was a large herd of swine feeding nearby on the mountain. The demons implored Him, saying, "Send us into the swine so that we may enter them." Jesus gave them permission. And coming out, the unclean spirits entered the swine; and the herd rushed down the steep bank into the sea, about two thousand of them; and they were drowned in the sea.

Their herdsmen ran away and reported it in the city and out in the country. And the people came to see what it was that had happened. They came to Jesus and observed the man who had been demon-possessed sitting down, clothed and in his right mind, the very man who had had the "legion"; and they became frightened. Those who had seen it described to them how it had happened to the demon-possessed man, and all about the swine. And they began to implore Him to leave their region. As He was getting into the boat, the man who had been demon-possessed was imploring Him that he might accompany Him. And He did not let him, but He said to him, "Go home to your people and report to them what great things the Lord has done for you, and how He had mercy on you." And he went away and began to proclaim in Decapolis what great things Jesus had done for him; and everyone was amazed. (Mark 5:1–20)

Discernment

This case study is full of movement. The man possessed by thousands of evil spirits comes eagerly from his tormented existence among the tombs to meet Jesus. Here is a principle in the ministry of Jesus worth noting: Jesus never sought out a demon; demons always came to Him. Let me emphasize this again: never go seeking for demons to cast out! In your ministry, if God wants you to pray for demonized individuals, allow God to send them to you. Many people have gotten themselves into deep trouble by going demon-hunting apart from divine, specific guidance of the Holy Spirit.

In this account, discernment of spirits is divided into two separate revelations regarding one individual. The first revelation identifies the ruling spirit by name and the second points to the condition of the man. As to the first movement in discernment of spirits, it would not be difficult for most of us to discern the obvious presence of evil spirits here. The man is breaking chains with supernatural strength and no one can keep him bound because there are so many spirits. The spirits have total control of the man's faculties. Additionally, the ruling spirit's own confession easily gives him away, as he speaks these words to Jesus: "What business do we have with each other, Jesus, Son of the Most High God?" (v. 7). The second movement in discernment deals with the level of agony within this man's soul. His inner struggle is filled with hatred, anger, and anguish. As I have already mentioned in this book, discernment of spirits operates within environment, within a short parameter. The revelation here is that evil has caused this man to lose all of his relationships, all of his reasoning, and all of his peace. A condition like this cannot be rationalized to be other or less than it is. Call it evil and treat evil accordingly.

Confirmation

When the man runs directly to Jesus and falls on his knees in front of Him, it confirms his condition. Notice that Jesus had already been saying, "Come out of the man, you unclean spirit!" (v. 8) before the man even identifies who Jesus is. The response of the spirits to Jesus Christ confirms that accurate and effective ministry is already happening. As you minister to people with serious problems, especially overseas, you are going to find that their hunger is greater than you expected. There is usually more faith in third-world countries than in churches within more developed countries. But there are spiritual problems of this nature everywhere! You must be careful in these situations. If you do not receive confirmation that you are on the right track, you could end up condemning someone instead of blessing someone.

Once I was preaching in a very affluent church. During my preaching, two things took place. To my right, in the back of the church, a man from the street fell to the floor and began to disrupt the service, making loud noises. He was crying and saying unintelligible words, which no one could understand. At almost the very same time, on the left side, a dignified man dressed in a beautiful, expensive suit fell on the floor and lay there, staring at the ceiling.

I remember it well. My first response was, *Why me?* I was all ready to preach a very nice sermon, and I was interested in doing well in this church. God must have had other ideas for this morning. I walked toward the back, but I still did not know what to do. I began to pray earnestly that God would tell me something—anything! I had to hear a revelation from the Lord. What I heard from Him was this, "Walk very slowly." So I walked slowly, taking in the predicament before me. The whole congregation became silent, with a few people whispering quietly. I directed my steps toward the disruptive man sprawled out on the floor to the right. The man looked filthy, as if he lived in the streets. His hair was long and soiled and his clothing had a distinct smell, to say the least. As I approached I could see that he was crying, tired of his life, yearning for someone to help him. I will never forget those eyes. Gradually I began to make out garbled words coming with painstaking effort from his lips: "Help! Jesus, help!"

I began to pray for him, and I realized this man was pure in heart, loved Jesus deeply, but was mentally impaired. I took his hands and asked him to repeat a simple prayer after me. As he responded, he began to cry much louder, saying, "Jesus, Jesus, Jesus," over and over. Here was a man in great need of love and acceptance. The pastors of the church came to minister to him, and I turned toward the man in the impeccable suit who was still lying on the floor to the left. It turns out that he was the one with the more serious spiritual problem. Darkness and evil had taken complete hold of his life. I prayed for him also.

What you assume at first can be deceiving, and that is what makes confirmation so vital. The man with a demon looked good. The other man was just a poor human being in tremendous frustration and pain, who had been perceived by the church as someone filled with evil. They were totally wrong. You have to hear the voice of God through discernment of spirits, and then ask for confirmation as you move. There is a huge difference between mental illness and evil.

Root Work

The root in the Gospel story of Mark 5:1–20 is bitterness. For many years, the man's problem has been with others. Those in the city have done all they knew to deal with him and, as a last resort, have brought him outside of the city to the caves and put chains on him. Anger, acidity, and poison fill this man's life. When someone has a relational need of bitterness, the consequences can become devastating. In situations where bitterness is the root, relationships are broken and damaged, seemingly beyond repair. Conflict, even to the point of extreme violence, is the norm. This man can't respond to or communicate with others. He has been in chains for a long time, and no one can subdue him. Even after his deliverance, when people from the nearby town first see him, they are afraid of him and they ask Jesus to leave their region. Bitterness, fueled with hatred and unforgiveness, dominates the scene. Bitterness is poison to the soul.

At times bitterness deforms the body. Men and women who hate do not look normal. In my years of traveling throughout churches in the United States and overseas I have found that bitterness is the most serious spiritual condition a man or woman can have. It affects their lives on all fronts. Hatred is a spiritual cancer that kills the body and distorts the personality.

Soul Ministry

"Seeing Jesus from a distance, he ran up and bowed down before Him; and shouting with a loud voice, he said, "What business do we have with each other, Jesus, Son of the Most High God? I implore You by God, do not torment me!" (vv. 6–7). These are the words of a desperate person who has been bound for a long time and who has abandoned all hope for deliverance from his circumstances. Ministry to the soul is that stage of ministry in which you hear the torment and agony of someone who is in despair, hoping for relief in his or her situation. The man runs to Jesus, bows before Him, and cries out loudly. The words he speaks sound rebellious and rejecting toward the Lord, but Jesus hears the deeper cry of his heart and moves toward him with compassion, which is urgently needed. Soul ministry is a time in which some form of conversation occurs in order to inform you about the heart of the individual, to consolidate discernment, and to provide clear direction for accurate prayer.

Command and Authority

As Jesus comes out of the boat, He is already speaking words of command and authority. The crisis is of such magnitude that the only correct response is to come against it with boldness and power. The words, "Come out of the man, you unclean spirit!" (v. 8) might not be the first move for most of us in ministry today, but it is effective and to the point. Jesus, through discernment, recognizes that this man is bound by evil and He deals with it without unnecessary delay. A demon occupies space and time within a human being. By space I mean that it takes over the mind and normal reasoning and robs the person of all peace. Time has to do with how long the individual has suffered and has remained bound and oppressed. The command here is simply, "Come out of the man." It could not be more clear and to the point.

Contact and Transmission

Contact and transmission is the act of releasing the healing power of God into a person. Throughout the Gospels, this is a consistent and repetitive movement of our Lord Jesus. In this event, Jesus makes His contact through dialogue. Since authority has already been established over the evil spirits, they are bound and submitted to Jesus. The same would be true for anyone who ministers using the powerful name of Jesus Christ.

Contact is made as Jesus begins the dialogue:

And He was asking him, "What is your name?" And he said to Him, "My name is Legion; for we are many." And he began to implore Him earnestly not to send them out of the country. Now there was a large herd of swine feeding nearby on the mountain. The demons implored Him, saying, "Send us into the swine so that we may enter them." Jesus gave them permission. And coming out, the unclean spirits entered the swine; and the herd rushed down the steep bank into the sea, about two thousand of them; and they were drowned in the sea. (vv. 9–13)

Remember that the object of ministry is the man, not the demons. Jesus is not impressed with demons and He has no interest in arguing with them. The evil spirits already know that they have lost their control over this man. When Jesus inquires, "What is your name?" He is speaking to the man, asking him his name. But the evil spirit in charge says, "My name is Legion, for we are many" (v. 9). The demons have been controlling him and speaking for him, and they continue to try to do so. Jesus gives the demons permission to go into the swine, pointing to the fact that Jesus is in complete authority. He does not negotiate or dialogue with evil spirits. Notice that this is the only attention Jesus gives to the demons.

Some Bible commentaries say that there were six thousand demons, as a Roman legion was made up of six thousand men. Other commentaries say two thousand. Whatever the number, the alienating of at least two thousand evil spirits and the death of the pigs releases this man completely! The man is totally restored to sanity and dignity and he immediately expresses a sincere and conscious desire to follow Jesus. However, the Master speaks another word of encouragement to him: "Go home to your people and report to them what great things the Lord has done for you, and how He had mercy on you" (v. 19). The man is actually commissioned by Jesus to bear witness to others regarding the power of the gospel. When our Lord gives His permission to the spirits to leave the man and go into the pigs, the power of God makes instant contact with the man's most desperate need. Jesus continues to transmit a blessing by calling forth a purpose for this man's life. Once a total outcast, despised and feared by all, he will now bear testimony in all of Decapolis of the life-changing power of Jesus Christ, the Son of God.

Check Around

"And he went away and began to proclaim in Decapolis what great things Jesus had done for him; and everyone was amazed" (v. 20). This miracle of deliverance will reach an entire region consisting of ten cities. A man wholly transformed and restored begins to testify with power and grace. The Lord's work this day is done. Time to move on.

14

Ministry to the Soul

A Renewed Spirit

D. L. Moody wrote, "The work of the Spirit is to impart life, to implant hope, to give liberty, to testify of Christ, to guide us into all truth, to teach us all things, to comfort the believer, and to convict the world of sin."[1]

Every human being who has been born again (regenerated by the Spirit of God) has a functioning spirit within him or her. This is the spirit of man.

> For who among men knows the thoughts of a man except the spirit of the man which is in him? Even so the thoughts of God no one knows except the Spirit of God. Now we have received, not the spirit of the world, but the Spirit who is from God, that we might know the things freely given to us by God. (1 Cor. 2:11–12)

The first work of the Holy Spirit is to cause the spirit of a man to come alive so that it is able to commune with God. "God is spirit, and those who worship Him must worship in spirit and truth" (John 4:24).

The new birth, or the spirit of man coming alive within him by the power of the Holy Spirit when he receives Jesus Christ as Lord and Savior, is the most miraculous reconstructive surgery ever performed by God. It is the beginning of an eternal spiritual journey. "But the one who joins himself to the Lord is one spirit with Him" (1 Cor. 6:17).

Body Preserved Complete

When we receive Jesus Christ as our Lord and Savior, we receive the Holy Spirit inside of us. Romans 8:15–16 says, "You have received a spirit of adoption as sons by which we cry out, 'Abba! Father!' The Spirit Himself testifies with our spirit that we are children of God." At the moment of salvation and forevermore, our renewed spirits are holy, perfect, and complete. The Holy Spirit becomes the seal or guarantee that God will redeem and restore the whole man, including the soul and eventually the body, in bodily resurrection. Ephesians 1:13–14 tells us that, "Having also believed, you were sealed in Him with the Holy Spirit of promise, who is given as a pledge of our inheritance, with a view to the redemption of God's own possession, to the praise of His glory." Sin brought a curse upon mankind, but the Holy Spirit who dwells within a believer is the promise—the pledge—that God will restore all that has been lost and will bring that person to wholeness!

Scripture tells us that the body of the believer is the temple of the living God. Further, we have the assurance that God's indwelling Spirit will continuously flow to heal the soul and body of the one in which He dwells until all is accomplished. The apostle Paul wrote in 1 Thessalonians 5:23, "Now may the God of peace Himself sanctify you entirely; and may your spirit and soul and body be preserved complete, without blame at the coming of our Lord Jesus Christ."

We have spent several chapters learning how discernment operates and is confirmed. Next, we looked carefully at the spiritual roots of rejection and rebellion, and the relational roots of unforgiveness and bitterness. We examined the seven consistent and repetitive movements of Jesus in an act of ministry. We are now ready to explore in more detail.

What Is Soul Ministry?

The soul is the part of man that requires healing and sanctification during the course of this earthly life. Soul ministry is conversational, creative, and personal. The most intimate need of a person is felt within the soul. However, it is not always easy for us to identify, because a human soul is complex, personal, and private. It can be difficult for the person receiving prayer to explain, because although she is suffering the consequences of life's difficulties, she may be incapable of identifying exactly what is causing so much pain, or she may want to hide what is deep inside because of fear or shame.

I call your attention once again to the reason for this book. In order to pray with accuracy for others, you cannot trust in popular psychology. You cannot depend upon the ability of hurting people to tell you where you should begin. You want to go to the place of the soul that requires healing, the way Jesus did. This means being able to hear the voice of God. This is why accurate prayer, guided by God, is so serious and wondrous. Think of it as God, the Holy Spirit, traveling within the innermost parts of someone to open a door that has been closed for a long time. Once He enters, He is able to convict, deliver, enlighten, and restore.

Until we grasp how to minister to the soul of man, our prayer will always be superficial. The soul makes up the singular identity and personality of an individual and will last forever, into eternity. The soul is what identifies us as to who we are. It's like your thumbprint— unique, personal, and unlike any other on the face of the earth. This is sobering when you realize that the human being in front of you willing to receive prayer is one of a kind. No one else is like this person. The mold was thrown away when God made him or her.

Only the Holy Spirit can fathom and penetrate the deepest level of the soul. Truly, without the guidance of the Holy Spirit it is impossible for anyone to discern within the soul. Medicine can quiet the mind, subduing the inner conflict, but when the soul is suffering only God can repair it. The Holy Spirit can do much better than all other efforts combined, since it was God Himself who created this individual in His own image. Three minutes of being touched by God can heal twenty years of struggling with identity.

In personal prayer, the main factor to consider is what direction the Holy Spirit wants to take as He moves within the innermost being of someone. For example, if discernment of spirits reveals that the need pertains to the individual's relationship with self or God (spiritual), this will point us toward a certain area of the soul. Likewise, if discernment reveals that the issue has to do with others (relational), this will lead us to target a different place within the soul. So, what actually comprises the soul, and how are we to know which area of the soul should be the focus of our prayer? Let's take a look.

What Comprises the Soul?

The English word translated "soul" comes from a Hebrew word, *nephesh*, meaning a breathing creature, person, self. The Hebrew concept of the soul is that it is the core, the heart, the unseen essence of a person, or the innermost self. When God created man, He "breathed into his nostrils the breath of life; and man became [*nephesh*] a living soul" (Gen. 2:7 KJV). There is a general understanding that the soul is comprised of three areas—mind, will, and emotions—those areas within us that know, decide, and feel. Let's briefly take a look at these three areas.

Mind

Your Intellect. The mind is a wonderful computer that utilizes data, learns, creates, and rationalizes with the speed of light. The mind remembers and recollects the past, and it processes the present. It is the totality of the conscious and unconscious mental functioning. Intellect is a processor and is different from feelings or willingness to do something or not to do it.

Scripture confirms the mind as being part of the soul. Psalm 139:14b states, "Wonderful are Your works, and my soul knows it very well." What the soul knows and understands deeply affects life. "For as he thinks [reckons] within himself [in his soul], so he is" (Prov. 23:7). You are what you think. "Immediately Jesus, aware in His spirit that they were reasoning that way within themselves, said to them, 'Why are you reasoning about these things within your hearts?'" (Mark 2:8). These examples point to the knowing, or the intellect of man.

Any prayer that is going to renew or enlighten the mind of someone else must be propelled by a revelation from God. Imagine you, with your brain, trying to communicate with someone whose mind or intellect is much superior to yours. What do you say to a mind who knows it all? How do you convince them of higher truth? How do you expose the area of greatest weakness, when they have all the answers? Do people who lean heavily on their intellect to approach life and who are highly educated wrestle with faith? Definitely. When an intellectual meets faith, very frequently a struggle is born. It is one thing to be educated about faith; it is another to experience a living and active faith when the mind is so dominant.

I met a gifted young man with many skills, including leading worship and teaching. Because of his impressive intellect, he began proving his point that he could create ministry by leading others into worship and teaching them what he knew.

The problem is that serving God begins with a call from God. You cannot assume a place of leadership in the body of Christ without a call. You can use your intellect and skill to start a company and sell products, but you cannot start a call and then expect that God will honor it.

This young man is an example of an intellectually driven person moving toward destruction. If God is not in it, the inevitable failure will end in discouragement. At present he is a frustrated young man, weak in his faith and hiding from God. However, an accurate prayer to confront the exaltation of his mind above simple trust in God could redirect his life back to Jesus Christ and His plan.

You are being called to encourage and to speak life and wholeness to a person who is bound up in his mind. How do you begin? Recall what we have studied about praying toward the need. If you discern unbelief, pray toward unbelief. If you discern pride, pray toward pride. If you discern confusion, pray toward confusion. What curtails the mind of this person is directly related to the inability to possess faith. It is a spiritual problem, a root of rejection of God (rebellion). The area of the soul that is most affected, which must yield to the working of the Holy Spirit, is the mind. Begin with the root that you discern, and you will arrive at the correct area of the soul.

"We are destroying speculations and every lofty thing raised up against the knowledge of God, and we are taking every thought captive to the obedience of Christ" (2 Cor. 10:5). If the root is a spiritual need of rejection of God (rebellion), the area of the soul that should be targeted for healing is the mind. The greatest need of the individual who lives in his mind is faith.

As I grew up, my father and my teachers could not give me faith, but they pointed me toward faith. I was intelligent, but it seemed that I had to experience failure and desperation in order to recognize that an active faith was the component that was lacking. I had to go through a process of forgetting everything that I thought I knew and allowing the Holy Spirit to propel me into a life of faith. Knowing about faith and living by faith are two separate things. The exaltation of intelligence is often the very thing that is blocking a living faith.

Will

The second area is the part of the soul that decides, determines, and moves forward. It is the God-given freedom to make your own decisions in life. This means that you can accept the person and work of the Holy Spirit or reject Him entirely. You are free to hear the voice of God or reject all intimacy with Him. This right to exercise your will determines how far you will go in God's plan for you. Sadly, you will meet many people locked into an eternal debate within themselves, who are never able to move forward in life.

The will is the faculty of conscious and deliberate action; the power of control that the mind has over its own actions. To decide and to choose is ever-present in our behavior. We are faced with choices in everything we do, all day long. Why would a soul have such an ingredient? It is because God wants you to respond to Him without coercion. To pray for the soul involves unlocking, opening, and creating a new perspective of life. Imagine your prayer releasing a soul to choose to bow down, to let go, and to be humble before God. What a blessing!

> I appeal to you therefore, brothers and sisters, by the mercies of God, to present your bodies as a living sacrifice, holy and acceptable to God, which is your spiritual worship. Do not be conformed to this world, but be transformed by the renewing of your minds, so that you may discern what is the will of God—what is good and acceptable and perfect. (Rom. 12:1–2 NRSV)

To discern the will of God requires a heart to hear and a desire to know His perfect will. At times people suffer anguish and heartache because they are struggling with their own will versus God's will. Job 7:14–15 says: "Then thou scarest me with dreams, and terrifiest me through visions, so that my soul chooseth strangling, and death rather than my life" (KJV). Job's terrible predicament was the loss of his family, possessions, and his physical health. He declares that his soul is choosing death over life because of the sorrow he is enduring. In Job 6:7 he insists that he is so distressed, he will not eat: "My soul refuses to touch them; they are like loathsome food to me."

How do you pray for someone such as Job, suffering as he wrestles with the will of God for his life? Would you call a counselor who would listen to Job's difficulties? We are in the age of referrals. Christians are calling on others to solve problems because they cannot discern the left hand from the right hand. God is equipping you to reach out to tortured souls, being confident that you have both Holy Spirit revelation and the Word of God on your side. Address your prayer to the area of need and something will break.

The psalmist also refers to the soul as will: "In the night my hand was stretched out without weariness; My soul refused to be comforted" (Ps. 77:2). How are you going to minister to the soul of this person? Speak to the will of man, reprimanding all anger and confusion. Speak to the will of man, releasing understanding and wisdom to hear God regarding His perfect will. Speak to the will of man, addressing anger, unforgiveness, hardness of heart, and self-determination that quenches the Holy Spirit of God. Speak to the will of man, commanding all resistance to bow down before the King of kings. Speak to the will of man to release forgiveness and kindness to family members. If the root is a relational root of unforgiveness or bitterness, the area of the soul that must be transformed is the will. The greatest need of that individual is a decision to let go of all control and hardness of heart; to yield and abandon everything he is holding so tightly into the hands of God.

Emotions

This third area of the soul is the part of us that feels emotions. These, of course, are the vast range of feelings experienced by all human beings. The emotions are an effective state of consciousness, which include happiness, love, excitement, sorrow, fear, anger, heartache, grief, and countless more sentiments.

In these four scriptures the soul rejoices, the soul grieves, the soul cries, and the soul trembles: "And my soul shall rejoice in the LORD" (Ps. 35:9). "My soul is deeply grieved, to the point of death" (Matt. 26:38). "My soul will sob in secret for such pride" (Jer. 13:17). "His soul trembles within him" (Isa. 15:4).

Accurate prayer that is directed toward emotional healing is not playing psychologist. It is not spiritualized psychotherapy or regression into the past. It is prayer led by the Holy Spirit, based upon the Word of God and faith. A vast array of areas within the emotions can become ill. Emotional disease can arise from extended grief, guilt, and mourning because of abortion, abandonment or neglect of a parent, sexual abuse by family members, and bullying and abuse by siblings, to name only a handful of scenarios.

The most beautiful aspect of accurate prayer led of the Holy Spirit is that He leads all the way. You do not have to be concerned about having a certain level of expertise about the human psyche. You don't need to read psychological journals. You must trust that you will not miss something or say the wrong thing. God is the One doing the healing, and He is faithful. He always leads when you call upon His name. That has been my experience of faith.

The soul has emotions that are hidden, hurt that has never been expressed, and heavy burdens not recognized, even by the person who carries them. Therefore, when you pray, use the basic root as your guide. For example, in the case of someone deeply rejected by their parents, you are probably going to target a spiritual need of rejection of self. As discernment of a root of rejection is confirmed, the prayer then moves toward the soul. Deal with the emotions, the area where the problem is found. If you arrive at this point there will be more revelation from God. Remember also that the heart of the matter is related not only to what sin has done in the life of the individual, but also in the whole family. It is at this stage of the prayer that a miracle can take place. Do not hurry here or pray a lot of words to fill space and time. Wait on the Lord, and He will come through for you.

No matter how diverse and different we might be, every man, woman, and child has one common problem: sin. While we might have different personalities, characters, or appearances, the soul is the same when it comes to sin, and God measures sin equally for all, with no respect of persons. There are no differences or shadows here as to a variety of souls. Humans are created by God. They are either joined to God as one spirit with Him or they are separated from God. This is why the scripture in Mark 12:28–31 makes everything so plain to us. Loving God with all of your heart, soul, mind, and strength, and loving your neighbor as yourself will fulfill the law of God, making it clear what the soul requires for wholeness. To whatever degree we fall short and are broken in those two areas, we are in need of healing and restoration.

When referring to the composition of the soul, one must see it not only as three parts, but as a campground full of life and activity. Whether you will be addressing mind, will, or emotions, seek to discern the root of the problem before you begin to pray. The Holy Spirit travels backward and forward to bring wholeness to someone's soul. It might seem like a simple concept to pray for a person and see healing occur within the soul. However, it is not simple to the Holy Spirit. When the apostle Paul writes of the Holy Spirit as the one who "searches all things" (1 Cor. 2:10), he is referring to the depth of the Holy Spirit in His ability to penetrate unreachable areas within a human being. A simple guided prayer releases the Holy Spirit to move into emotions that may have been damaged twenty years earlier. It can bring freedom to a mind bound in rationalized thinking and working with a will set against the purposes of God. If you are still with me this far into this book, you may be realizing that praying with accuracy goes much deeper than you ever thought. Prayer that is accurate hears the voice of God much louder than any preconceived ideas or your personal opinion.

Jesus' Ministry to the Soul

If you follow the Spirit of God in ministry, you will see Him moving in the soul of someone with the same kind of precision and accuracy as a surgeon would in the operating room. You need to know where to go and what to do when you get there, and then you must complete your task before getting out. It would be good for us to look at an example in the ministry of Jesus found in John 5:1–9. This account will help us to see Jesus operating within the soul of a man in a perfect act of ministry.

> After these things there was a feast of the Jews, and Jesus went up to Jerusalem.
>
> Now there is in Jerusalem by the sheep gate a pool, which is called in Hebrew Bethesda, having five porticoes. In these lay a multitude of those who were sick, blind, lame, and withered, [waiting for a moving of the waters; for an angel of the Lord went down at certain seasons into the pool and stirred

up the water; whoever then first, after the stirring up of the water, stepped in was made well from whatever disease with which he was afflicted.] A man was there who had been thirty-eight years. When Jesus saw him lying there, and knew that he had already been a long time in that condition, He said to him, "Do you wish to get well?" (vv. 1–6)

A variety of serious conditions were present at this pool of Bethesda. There were the sick, the blind, the lame, and the withered, or paralyzed. It is interesting to note the kinds and degrees of infirmities represented by these groups. The blind are fully able to move their bodies, but are hindered by lack of vision. The sick and the lame also are able to move to a certain degree, but are restricted in their movements. Finally, those who are paralyzed are impaired and debilitated altogether, having no movement at all. This is the environment in which Jesus finds Himself. In the midst of so much suffering, the object of ministry for Jesus on this particular day is a man restricted from any movement, since he had been a paralytic for thirty-eight years. Because he knew himself to be a paralytic, he could not think of himself as otherwise. His identity was wrapped up in being a paralytic, and the life he lived as such. His soul contributed to his paralysis. His mind knew it, his will accepted it, and his emotions felt it deeply within.

How is the root or core need related to the man's paralysis? We have here a case of constant rejection, because the lifestyle of a paralytic dictated poverty and shame. For thirty-eight years, he had been constrained to lie motionless, begging and depending upon others for his livelihood. Jesus asked the man a pointed question, "Do you wish to get well?" in order to hear him confess the desire of his heart. Jesus moves the man out of a past characterized by a root of rejection into the present reality with His question. By asking him, "Do you wish to get well?" He is saying to the man, in essence, "Today is your day. You can choose what you want." Here Jesus is allowing the man to make a choice based on freedom, which is a basic desire of every soul.

The point we are trying to identify here is exactly when the Holy Spirit began to minister within this man's soul. At what point did Jesus apply some pressure? When acute rejection exists in someone's life, you must detect it and move quickly into the area of the soul that begs for the most help. It is clear that Jesus went to the emotions of the paralytic. Through His question, He gives the man a choice. How long had it been since this man had a choice about anything? Jesus allows the man to feel like a human being again by having the ability to express a desire, which would raise his self-esteem. Approaching this rejected and helpless person with a question allows the man to decide what he really wants for his life. It communicates that the man has value, worth, and is not overlooked by God.

Ministry to the soul, therefore, must bring the person out of his or her misery and provide a breath of fresh air. In the ministry of Jesus, we see this methodology in nearly all of the miracles. When life is paralyzed, you find influences that have been compounded, one upon another, and they must be addressed. Jesus sees that the paralysis exists not only in the man's body, but in his soul as well. This man needs to be given an opportunity to exercise faith and movement within his soul in order to experience healing and wholeness in his body.

> The sick man answered Him, "Sir, I have no man to put me into the pool when the water is stirred up, but while I am coming, another steps down before me." Jesus said to him, "Get up, pick up your pallet and walk." Immediately the man became well, and picked up his pallet and began to walk. (John 5:7–9)

The man's response to Jesus' question is, "Yes, I want to be healed." But there is a much more complex problem that has to be solved.

When the water moves, his perception of his life is that he has no one to help him into the water. The man's passive and habitual dependency upon others has compounded his physical condition. He has spent many years viewing others as obstacles who have prevented him from receiving healing. He has taken on the role of a helpless victim, and defines himself as such.

Jesus detects all of this and moves into the soul realm with power and authority. Jesus says, "Get up, pick up your pallet and walk" (v. 8). The root is rejection. The obvious physical and practical need here is the ability to walk. But the area of the soul that is crying for a touch from God is the man's emotions. When he realizes that he is being offered a choice about his life, probably for the first time in many years, his hope springs to life and his faith rises to the occasion. The man stands upright, healed in body, but healed even more profoundly in his inner man.

The soul is a hive of activity that only the hand of God can put into order. The soul does not create the root; it only feeds upon it and keeps it entrenched in someone's life. When praying for someone, be aware that it is the soul that feels many feelings and holds on to memories and habits. The soul fights the spirit and also receives the spirit (see Galatians 5:17). The soul reasons, cries, suffers, asks, and chooses. When you pray, your job is to minister to the soul based on knowledge given to you by the Holy Spirit. A successful prayer never begins in the soul. A successful prayer ends in the soul.

The Door

Let's review the process of ministry to the soul a little bit. As you begin to pray, you want to first identify if the need before you is spiritual or relational. I call this point "the door." For our purposes, let us call the left door "spiritual" and the right door "relational."

If you are led by the Holy Spirit and the application of the Word to enter the left door, you next have to choose from two areas: rejection of self or rejection of God (rebellion). In the same way, if you pass through the right door, a relational root will lead to either unforgiveness or bitterness. Now I want you to see how great a progression your prayer has already taken. Discernment of the correct door means you are already 90 percent accurate in your prayer. You are in the kitchen!

Determining the direction to go will come to you more easily after you reach this point. If you are praying for someone with a relational root of unforgiveness, ministry to the soul will deal with this person's will or disposition. On the other hand, if you discover a spiritual problem of rebellion, the ramifications of rebellion such as intellectualism, pride, and rationalization will soon be exposed. Are you seeing how the identification of the root flows into the next step—ministry to the soul?

Here is an example of a prayer for someone who is deeply rejected:

Lord, thank You for Your love displayed on the cross of Calvary. By the power of Your love poured out on the cross, heal the most intimate parts of my sister's emotions. Remove from her the idea of not being important, of not belonging, having no value, or not counting in the scheme of things.

You identify the root and move quickly to the part of the soul that is suffering most. Another prayer here could be:

God, in the power of the Spirit, I sever all rejection and timidity. I speak to all emotions that have diminished a

sense of worth and confidence in who You created her to be.
I release my sister from uncertainty, inferiority, insecurity,
timidity, and shyness.

These are issues of the soul related to rejection, which have kept this individual blind, lame, or paralyzed in life and relationships.

Prayer that targets someone's disposition or will is related to a root of unforgiveness or a root of bitterness. The will of a person is his or her determination to stand for something or fight for an idea. The will of man always affects the relational part of someone's life. Will is both the king and the queen of relationships. Whenever there are "others" and "you," the will establishes its place and fights for identity. A prayer for unforgiveness or bitterness may be along these lines:

Lord, I come against all schemes of hate and disdain toward others. Remove all thoughts of retaliation, and cleanse my brother's soul this very moment. In the name of Jesus Christ, I call for reconciliation and peace in this family. Thank You that You took all hatred and wrath upon Yourself on the cross so that we can have peace. I speak against hardness of heart, strong will, disagreement, envy, and strife. Come, Holy Spirit, and undo these arguments and all discord.

Here you are directly taking authority against a strong will and ministering to the soul.

These prayers are simply guidelines. The Holy Spirit must show you how to pray for each individual in each instance. However, the principle here is that as the Holy Spirit gives revelation about the root problem in someone's life, there will be a strong indicator of where healing and freedom is needed within the areas of the soul.

Consequences

The next stage of prayer must deal with the consequences. The issues of the soul, deep within the heart, translate into outer ramifications, which are tangible and urgent. Here, you are dealing with specific consequences this person is having as a result of his or her core need. Deep-seated rejection very often leads to sexual confusion and difficulties. Therefore, forgiveness, cleansing, and a new start in this area will be required.

Passivity, withdrawal, loneliness, and heaviness also come out of rejection, and may be holding the person back from pursuing fulfillment in life and ministry. When the will is involved, hardness, harshness, bitterness, acridity, and poison in the soul may have stolen joy and damaged relationships. If someone is experiencing trouble in the family, you address these issues. If someone is holding onto hatred toward others, there is almost certainly a breakdown of specific relationships. Deliberate action must be taken to begin the process of restoration.

When it comes to the area of the mind, you will meet those who cannot cry, cannot love, cannot sing, and cannot praise. These individuals often rationalize the minutest of details pertaining to faith in Jesus Christ and are plagued by doubt in matters of belief and surrender. Then there are those who will not accept the way others worship and express their faith, adhering to tradition and refusing to compromise or meet someone halfway. This stage is where prayer becomes very practical. What is being hindered in the person's life? Where has the condition of blindness, lameness, or paralysis set in? Is it in the area of finances, family relationships, sexual balance, or employment? Is the issue affecting church relationships and ministry? Where does real and lasting change have to occur in order to reflect healing of the soul?

In the case of the man at the pool of Bethesda, he has long given up on himself as a human being who has any choices regarding his life. His practical need is to walk, but the underlying plight of his soul is to know that he can choose dignity and wholeness instead of being a helpless, dependent victim. Once the matter of the soul is identified, Jesus then presses the man to the practical application. That is, the man is challenged to begin to move, to exert energy in order to physically rise and pick up his pallet. When the prayer reaches this stage, there is always some sort of practical and specific application that requires movement of some kind: physical movement, agreeing to meet up with an estranged family member, extending an act of kindness toward someone, changing jobs, or forgiving someone a debt.

Ministry to the soul in the consistent and repetitive methodology of Jesus is that moment when the person He touched knows that life is going to be different from that moment on. Engaging the soul of the person for whom you are praying means that they play a certain part in their own healing. They receive the dealings of the Holy Spirit and allow the eyes, the heart, or the volition of their will to be opened to new possibilities. They press through to do something they never thought they could. It is a critical moment, which may be long remembered by the one whom God has placed in your path so that you might pray—with accuracy—for him or her.

15

The Ethics of Prayer

The ethics of prayer addresses good protocol—the manner in which one conducts prayer for others. Accurate prayer and ethics are mutually dependent if you hope to have an effective ministry. When the Holy Spirit reveals personal information to you about someone in need, especially in a public setting, you must be sensitive to how it is going to affect the person receiving prayer. This is something that must be studied, developed, and applied. It is a matter of cooperation with the work of the Holy Spirit. In most cases, when you practice good prayer ethics, the Holy Spirit will honor you and continue to show more to you. Observance of good prayer ethics means that you are acting to benefit the person above yourself and to glorify God. In this chapter on ethics, we will discuss several topics: semantics, sanctity, environment, interaction, gender factors, bedside manner, waiting, and the altar.

Semantics

As much as possible, the words you employ when you pray for someone have to be chosen wisely. Though you may be praying accurately according to the discernment you are receiving from the Lord, if you use improper wording, you can be grossly misunderstood. Careless use of words can damage the outcome of your time of ministry and can hinder the work of the Holy Spirit.

We have by this point learned so much about the four basic needs or roots of rejection, rebellion, unforgiveness, and bitterness. We have seen that a root is the core area where prayer for wholeness should begin. It is where the Holy Spirit will concentrate and impart knowledge with which to formulate a prayer that is accurate and effective. However, these root words should primarily be for your understanding as you minister, and are not necessarily to be spoken in the actual prayer.

As you discern and receive information from the Holy Spirit, the manner in which you convey it will deeply affect the person before you. Thus, at this holy and momentous time, your words must be uttered under the anointing of the Holy Spirit after carefully listening to God. It is here that miracles begin to happen and conviction takes place right before your eyes. Here is where the faithful ones will hear from God.

When you are praying for someone pertaining to his or her basic need, it is advisable to find words that will describe the situation before you without actually using the four terms of *rejection, rebellion, unforgiveness,* and *bitterness.* For example, *timidity, shyness, ineptness, withdrawal, insecurity, inferiority,* and *inadequacy* are fitting words to be used in prayer when rejection of self exists. These are only a few words I give as an example of how to treat rejection of self in prayer. Words such as these are specific and personal and cause the person to know that he or she is known and understood by God.

I can remember a time when I prayed for someone using the word *shyness,* but the moment called for a better word and I could not think of it. I explained to the person what I was discerning as I prayed. "God, remove any insecurity in this woman, any fear of being shut out or shunned by others, any idea that she does not belong. Help her to not feel invisible or unimportant in the midst of others." You notice that the word *rejection* is not mentioned. By using phrases that describe very specifically the reality she is dealing with day to day, you are able to get to the heart of the need. Because you are acting gently and thoughtfully, you will find that revelation increases as you speak and the prayer is being readily received.

The same would apply when addressing a root of rebellion. *Rebellion* is a strong word, which in many instances will bring offense to the person listening. A growing Christian who is trying his best to build his faith does not want to be told that he is rebellious. Keep in mind that rebellion may be a condition of his soul that is, as of yet, untreated by the Holy Spirit. If derivatives of this word are used, your tactfulness may result in greater acceptance of your prayer. Remember that the goal is to formulate a prayer led by the Holy Spirit, which will bring about conviction, healing, and wholeness.

Here are some of the words or phrases that pertain to a root of rebellion: *thoughts that diminish the presence of God, self-will, disobedience, intellectualization, rationalization, perfectionism, worry, fear,* and *anxiety.* Rebellion is something that develops when rejection of self is untreated or ignored. As we have learned, rejection of self can produce rebellion toward God. One example would be a young female student who feels so rejected by others, she begins to develop an attitude toward God. She starts to blame God for her pain. Thoughts continue to rise up in her mind against God because of being rejected by others. Eventually, she cannot hear the Lord because she is so absorbed with the rationalization that constantly goes on in her mind. Her mind is in control and she is trying to solve a spiritual problem by thinking her way out instead of receiving conviction and truth from the Holy Spirit.

Another word that carries forth the essence of rebellion is *perfectionism.* This dominates someone's life when everything must be perfect with a drive to perform for God or receive approval from others. Perfectionism causes worry, fear, and anxiety because the pressure to perform only increases. Good is never good enough. It is not sufficient to do well—the person has to outdo others and create a feeling of superiority in order to feel safe. Someone who is rejected will reject himself, and when this is not dealt with he will reject the acceptance and grace of God. Needing somehow to earn or achieve acceptance from God, he falls into the bondage of perfectionism. This issue has been compounded by much fear and anxiety and thoughts that are locked in. Thus, the use of the word *rebellion* is not necessarily encouraged here.

What we are trying to pinpoint is the constant battle that the specific root has caused in a person's life. Our hope is to deal with the product or the effects of that root in prayer under the power of the Holy Spirit. To simply call a person "rebellious" can come across as an indictment. You don't want to put anyone down or label them. You want to hit upon the daily struggle that goes on in the soul. Following the leading of the Holy Spirit, when you are able to articulate the conflict in the heart of this person, the chances are high that conviction will be the result. The person may feel that, for the first time, they are known and understood by God in an intimate way. This conviction causes the door of his or her heart, which has formerly been locked, to open up and become willing to receive ministry. Therefore, the intentional use of the right words in prayer can greatly affect the outcome. Romans 2:4 says, "Or do you think lightly of the riches of His kindness and forbearance and patience, not knowing that the kindness of God leads you to repentance?"

If there is an area where you must be tactful and prudent in your choice of words, it is when you are dealing with a relational issue. This requires gracious and thoughtful words as you pray for someone, because the difficulty began with others and concerns others in past and present relationships. Because of the very nature of the problem, the one with a relational need is more prone to be easily offended by what you try to say. Even though you know that you have good motives, your prayer is going to be better received if you can use tactful words.

When praying for someone deeply affected by unforgiveness or bitterness, one may use words or phrases to this effect: *extended grief, condemnation, accusation, strife, resentment, heaviness, depression, guilt, distrust, paranoia, anger,* or *retaliation.* If you examine the language here you can see that each word is pointing toward a very specific area. For example, if you use the phrase "extended grief" when praying for someone who lost a loved one and remains grieving for many years, you are dealing with an underlying matter of unforgiveness. Perhaps this person is holding back an unresolved grudge and cannot release the departed to rest in peace. In our churches, I often find a large group of elderly members who still mourn for loved ones long beyond the normal three years needed for healing. I have seen some individuals mourning for thirty or forty years, filled with mental anguish and unrest. In some churches, the people communicate with the dead better than they communicate with the living! Your prayer for someone who cannot pass through grief is one of the most precious and sensitive moments you will experience in your ministry. Never forget that the Holy Spirit is the Comforter, and that in these situations He will make His presence known in a powerful way. How do you make the words work for you in this case? When praying for a widow who lost her husband twenty years ago, say words like the following:

God, heal the past wounds in this family. Remove all resentment that might create sadness that won't go away. Holy

> Spirit, remove any memory of the past that remains as real
> as if it were yesterday. Help my sister to fully let go of any
> regrets and know that she is free to move on and rejoin life.
> Today, heal all hurts that have been left in her heart.

———————————————

Unforgiveness is not mentioned in the prayer by intention. But it is the underlying issue. The Holy Spirit will be there to help you formulate words that minister to the deepest hurt and target the bondage. When the Holy Spirit convicts, He is not accusing or condemning. He is there to set people free from what has been holding on to them for so long. As we do the ministry of Jesus, the words we use may be bold, but also must be full of His love and sensitivity to the soul in front of us.

Below is a further list of related terms that can be used in formulating a powerful prayer. As you read these words, try to create a concept for each one of them. Each is related to a root. However, these words are also part of a whole and can be interrelated and used in relation to more than one root. Familiarity with these words will help you make contact with the specific problem as you listen to what the Holy Spirit is saying.

Spiritual Need: Rejection

Insecurity: inferiority, self-pity, loneliness, timidity, shyness, inadequacy, ineptness

Depression: despair, despondency, discouragement, defeatism, dejection, hopelessness, suicide, death, morbidity

Passivity: indifference, listlessness, lethargy

Withdrawal: daydreaming, pretension, unreality, escape

Spiritual Need: Rebellion

Accusation: judging, criticism, fault-finding, blame, pride

Control: possessiveness, dominance, manipulation, intimidation

Impatience: agitation, frustration, intolerance

Mental Illness: fear, lies, insanity, scenarios, paranoia, hallucinations

Nervousness: tension, anxiety, worry, temper, restlessness, insomnia

Relational Need: Unforgiveness

Anger: resentment, dissention, temper, conflict, enmity

Paranoia: jealousy, envy, suspicion, distrust, persecution, fears

Covetousness: discontent, ingratitude, greed

Grief: sorrow, heartache, crying, sadness, heartbreak, heaviness

Guilt: shame, condemnation, pain

Relational Need: Bitterness

Retaliation: destruction, spite, hatred, hurt, cruelty, vengeance, poison

Strife: contention, bickering, argument, quarreling, fighting

Hopelessness: hardness, joyless, cynicism

Sanctity

It is not only what you say that validates your ministry to an individual; it is who you are in his or her eyes. Thus, your personal prayer life is directly connected to the way you pray for others. Without communion with God, you cannot help anyone else restore his or her own communion with God.

E. M. Bounds wrote:

> The soul which has come into intimate contact with God in the silence of the prayer-chamber is never out of conscious touch with the Father. . . . the heart is always going out to him in loving communion, and . . . the moment the mind is released from the task on which it is engaged, it returns as naturally to God as the bird does to its nest.[1]

Intimacy with God will open doors for your prayers to be powerful and effective. Intimacy with God produces love for His people. Without love, you become a tinkling cymbal. If pride is in your life, you will not hear from the Holy Spirit. It takes a very humble person to be able to pray for others. In my life, I have never changed people by praying for them. God has done all of the changing and the healing. What is so wonderful and merciful about our Father is that if you have the right heart, He will use you to minister to others even when you do not feel like you are ready to do so. My part and your part are very small, and yet important. Prayer is not a business; it is a way we serve God's people.

I suggest that your prayer life be a fasted life also. For a period of time, from midnight Thursday to midnight Sunday, I strongly recommend that you fast for your prayer ministry. Give priority to this, and you will see fruits that will bless your life in church and out of church. The purpose of fasting is to hear the voice of God. The first day, you will feel tired and hungry. The second day, your body will begin to be cleansed and energized. The third day, a quietness will overcome you— enabling you to hear Him. What you hear from God on the third day of fasting will minister to your spirit and build your body. Strength will come and enable you to hear God more clearly. It only takes one word from the Lord to produce a wonderful change inside of you.

David said of his fasting life: "But as for me, when they were sick, my clothing was sackcloth: I humbled my soul with fasting, and my prayer kept returning to my bosom" (Ps. 35:13). David's prayers returned to strengthen his heart after humbling his soul before God in prayer for his enemies. I have never seen a man or woman full of pride who has a vital prayer life. A prideful man or woman is self-sufficient and has a strong will. But coming to God with selfishness and ulterior motives will not produce results. The prophet Isaiah said: "Behold, you fast for contention and strife and to strike with a wicked fist. You do not fast like you do today to make your voice heard on high" (Isa. 58:4).

Andrew Murray, describing the immeasurable value of humility, wrote this: "Here is the path to the higher life. Down, lower down! . . . Just as water ever seeks and fills the lowest place, so the moment God finds men abased and empty, His glory and power flow in to exalt and bless."[2]

Environment

Effectiveness in prayer is directly connected to the environment. Jesus gave detailed attention to environment every time He ministered. Most of us would not think that the mental and spiritual condition of other people present would interfere with our ability to effectively hear God and carry out our ministry. Nevertheless, the ethics of accurate prayer require careful assessment of the environment, including those who are present and their spiritual condition.

In my years of serving the Lord, I at times ignored the environment when praying for someone. But I have learned that balance and order must be established and distractions and interruptions managed before you begin to pray. If possible, the place you choose to minister to someone should be separated and consecrated to God for the purpose of prayer. In a church setting, the church parlor or a quiet office or classroom is best. Try to arrange for someone from the congregation to be present with you at all times. This is better—and more ethical—than praying alone with anyone. If you are going to a home, have a member of the family present or bring the local pastor along. Those who minister to others must take steps to create an environment for prayer and to establish a demeanor that invites others to trust them for who they are in the community of faith.

Let's take a look at how the ethics demonstrated by Jesus placed importance upon environment. In Luke 8:40–56, Jesus meets Jairus, the synagogue ruler, and decides to go to his house. As Jesus approaches the house, someone comes out and announces to Jairus that his little girl is dead, saying, "Your daughter has died; do not trouble the Teacher any more" (v. 49). Jesus, on hearing this, says emphatically to Jairus, "Do not be afraid any longer; only believe, and she will be made well" (v. 50). This is an excellent example of how to deal with unbelief in the environment. Sometimes as you begin to pray for someone, you almost can hear unbelief coming from all sides. Usually, I look around just to see who is nearby or who is waiting to be next in the line of prayer. At times, I have taken the person aside and prayed for him or her without anyone being close enough to hear.

In this instance, when Jesus hears a negative word that could derail Jairus's faith, He immediately turns to Jairus and responds with a positive faith statement: "Do not be afraid." These words are spoken to Jairus at a vulnerable moment, just when he is about to come into his house and see his little daughter. You have to attend to the moment to empathize with the degree of tension and anxiety that was present within Jairus. He is experiencing powerful emotions that surface only in the gravest of occasions. It is critical for Jairus to hear this positive word so that his faith will be encouraged. Yes, what you say in a prayer setting can influence the outcome!

When Jesus comes into the house of Jairus, He allows no one else to enter except Peter, James, John, Jairus, and his wife. We are accustomed to assume that He allowed these three disciples because they were the closest to Him in ministry. I prefer to think that their level of faith played the predominant role here. In some translations, Luke 8:54 begins with this statement: "And He put them all out . . ." This indicates that Jesus deliberately removed anyone who lacked faith or who was emotionally distraught about losing the little girl. Those whom Jesus permitted to remain inside of the house had to believe for the life of this child. If environment and who was a part of it during the act of praying was a relevant factor in the ministry of our Lord, then we would do well to heed this principle for ourselves as well.

As I go to minister in churches as an evangelist, it has become my habit to take a very careful look at who is present. At times, the congregation is more than willing to receive, but the pastor seems to be reserved and guarded. I know that I am going to have to deal with unbelief even before I bring the Word for the morning service. It's easy to feel discouraged when you sense so much resistance to the person and the work of the Holy Spirit. But there are things you can do, such as singing a song or giving a testimony, which can prepare cautious hearts to open up to the Word and the work of the Holy Spirit.

The same is true in personal prayer for others. Is the environment peaceful, or is there tension in the air? Pay attention to the person's hands. Nervousness and agitated hands can tell you what is going on inside of someone's mind. At times, I delay the prayer a bit and say something about the weather, some good food I recently had, or a sporting event. I will smile and tell them something about myself before beginning to minister. You will have to, at times, make a comment or two that are completely unrelated to the prayer to follow.

This helps the person to relax and relate to you. Keep your eyes open and register their response via voice, intonation, fidgeting, or stiffness of the body. All the while you are awaiting the moment when the Holy Spirit can break through with a word of wisdom or knowledge to help you begin your prayer.

When I want to take the pulse of a church, I observe those who serve in the environment regularly, such as ushers. Those who serve within the sanctuary are good gauges of what makes up the environment. When they seem to just stare at you, or they are sitting listlessly during the beginning of the service, it tells me they are in need themselves. If those who serve are in an unhealthy condition, I know that the congregation is in even worse need. Observe the furniture to see if it's showing wear and tear, and look under the pulpit for trash. Is there furniture in front of the altar rail? Plastic flowers in the altar area indicate that no one wants to take care of real flowers. Old hymn books laying about and dirty floors indicate that no one is cleaning the church. If you see old and dirty furniture collecting dust, you also will feel the spiritual pulse of the environment. People begin to look like their environment when they are not receiving prayer or attention from the pastor.

Life is present in the environment when children run in the sanctuary; flowers are alive and breathing; music is creative and engaging; the altar rail has inviting pads for those who want to kneel in prayer; the parking lot looks repaired, and the bathrooms are clean. Life is present when the janitor is smiling; the piano player is playing something inspiring; and people are shaking hands, hugging, and welcoming each other. All of these things are signs that the environment is busy and full of hope for the morning or evening service.

In Mark 9:14–29, Jesus comes to the scene to minister to a father and his son, who is possessed by an evil spirit. As the story opens, the crowd has been watching the disciples unsuccessfully try to cast the evil spirit out of the boy. It is an environment filled with strife and chaos. Jesus removes the father and the boy from the midst of the clamoring multitude and takes them into a more controlled environment, where He speaks confidentially to the father. A few verses later, as Jesus sees the crowd pressing toward them once again, He moves quickly to minister deliverance to the boy, rebuking the evil spirit. Jesus does not allow the ministry of deliverance to become a public spectacle. His approach of ministering apart from the crowd grants dignity to the boy and his father.

This story is a powerful example to us, revealing the heart of God toward people who are troubled and misunderstood. Whenever possible, our manner of interacting with such individuals should reflect the ethics demonstrated by Jesus so as to not draw undue attention to the person or to ourselves. Another example of the importance of environment occurs in Mark 8:22–26. Here, Jesus finds it necessary to physically take the person away from the village where he lives. Once away from the village, Jesus performs a miracle of healing using a most unusual method:

> And they came to Bethsaida. And they brought a blind man
> to Jesus and implored Him to touch him. Taking the blind
> man by the hand, He brought him out of the village; and after
> spitting on his eyes and laying His hands upon him, He asked
> him, "Do you see anything?" And he looked up and said, "I
> see men, for I see them like trees, walking around." Then again
> He laid His hands on his eyes; and he looked intently and was
> restored, and began to see everything clearly. And He sent
> him to his home, saying, "Do not even enter the village."

Spitting on the man's eyes might not seem to demonstrate superb ethics, but no one should question this act of Jesus as being out of order. Ethics such as these are required when nothing else will suffice. One of the main ingredients of any miracle is something that will generate faith. As you read all of the miracles of Jesus, it is clear that this is a unique situation for a couple of reasons. First, Jesus is not creating a formula for a spit ministry. But in this particular case, Jesus uses His own saliva instead of oil to bring healing to the man. Second, notice how Jesus relates to the blind man—personally taking him by the hand and leading him completely outside of the city before He begins to minister to him. This also is unique. Why did Jesus feel this was necessary?

We read in Matthew 11:20–21 that Bethsaida was one of the three towns reproached by Jesus for their overt unbelief. This little fishing village close to the Sea of Galilee was filled with hard, unbelieving hearts. Our Lord is not about to allow this evil environment of unbelief to rob the blind man of his healing. Jesus therefore employs a methodology that first removes the man from the environment of the town, outside of the city gate. He then does something rather startling, perhaps to shock the man into belief. As we closely observe the ethics of Jesus throughout the Gospels, we see that He repeatedly deals with and takes action to create an environment necessary for a miracle to take place. In other words, you cannot just succumb to whatever environment exists. There are times when God may lead you to create environment by taking intentional, even unusual, steps which will open the way for the Holy Spirit to move.

Interaction

Interaction, which prepares the way for prayer, begins as soon as you arrive at the church or the gathering. Someone who ministers in prayer should be reaching out to everyone, including the leaders and the staff members. Your attitude in these moments is a testimony of humility and servanthood. In the act of taking time to listen, care, and love, you will find that the walls are coming down and you are receiving acceptance from those you hope to reach. The spirit of a servant must be proven before people will open their hearts to receive prayer. The best involvement with the congregation begins in odd places, be it in the parking lot of the church or outside of the bathroom. I prefer to arrive thirty minutes early to every service just to be there as people are coming in. In this way, when it comes time to pray, I already have a sense of those who have the greatest needs and they already feel comfortable with me.

Gender Factors

Principles involving gender raise some of the most sensitive issues in prayer ministry. While a man praying for a woman or a woman praying for a man does not diminish the power of prayer, it does have some bearing upon the approach one must use. When confronted with the needs of women—including deep rejection from husbands and men in general—a man should extend extra gentleness, which requires a more gracious choice of language and better manners in prayer. If you follow the ministry of Jesus, you will observe that His behavior was exceptionally sensitive to women, who were not only rejected but also ostracized in the society of His day. Unfortunately, women are still rejected today in much of society as well as in the home.

In Luke 8:42b–48, a woman who had had a flow of blood for twelve years approaches Jesus. Coming from behind Him, she touches the hem of His garment and her flow of blood stops at once. As Jesus insists upon knowing who has touched Him and the disciples try to argue with Him, the woman sees that she cannot escape unnoticed and falls at the feet of Jesus. There is definitely a moment of waiting upon her to present herself by coming forward. This is unlike any of the other miracles of Jesus. He is dealing here with a woman with a delicate problem and His kindness is reflected in the passage. He even says to her, "Daughter, your faith has made you well; go in peace" (v. 48). Considering the lowly role of women in that time and culture, Jesus models an affectionate, respectful, and caring way of dealing with this woman, which is revolutionary.

Many years ago, a woman came to the altar for prayer at the close of a Sunday morning service. Immediately, the Holy Spirit made it inarguably clear to me that I was not to touch her at all—not even a handshake to introduce myself. After a few minutes of prayer for her, I heard a word from God. The word was *blood*. That single word told me that something very serious had happened, so I asked her when the infraction had occurred. She responded that she had been physically and sexually assaulted by a man the night before and that she was traumatized. A touch from any man during this vulnerable time would have caused her further turmoil and the Holy Spirit knew this. As her tears flowed, I dismissed the congregation and called several older women from the church to come up and surround her. The emergency had to be dealt with, but because of the nature of the crime against her, it called for extraordinary discretion and privacy.

Another time, at a church service in Brazil, a street woman came to the altar. She was improperly dressed but was desperately seeking help from God. I knew that the Lord wanted her to be shielded from the curious attention of many eyes watching her. Yet I could not get involved in prayer or hear from the Holy Spirit for her life until she was covered. I placed my jacket around her so that she would feel safe and more relaxed to receive prayer from me. The Lord touched her life that night. A little sensitivity can go a long way.

As a man praying for a woman, you must gauge your position if she is sitting or kneeling and you are standing, looking down at her. Be sensitive as to how a woman feels having a man standing above her. When the occasion calls for it, you should lower yourself down to her level, without kneeling. This will produce less self-consciousness for her and a feeling of trust, and your prayer will flow without distraction. It's a simple thing like this that can make a huge difference.

Even though your methodology may not change in general, awareness regarding factors of gender will help your prayer ministry to be more free and effective. Of the thirty-seven miracles of Jesus recorded in the Gospels, five of them involve women as the principle subject. In each account, you will find that our Lord demonstrates a more careful treatment and consideration of women. His ethics in ministry when it comes to gender issues are the highest to be found anywhere.

Don't hold back in prayer just because the person is of the opposite sex. Even so, in special situations, try to have someone remain with you as you pray. When accurate prayer hits the target, it can bring strong memories, emotions, and reactions to the surface. I advise that if you are a man praying for a woman, ask another woman who understands prayer to stay nearby. If the subject matter must remain confidential, the woman can remain just outside of the door, praying. But if the conversation and prayer involves sexuality, it is better to have someone else in the room with you. Ethics in these cases must be carefully observed. Even given this word of caution, do not avoid dealing with a delicate problem. Many of God's people have serious difficulties in the sexual arena and you cannot shy away from ministering to them. They need help that only the Holy Spirit can give. Still, always use wisdom and employ good ethics when this kind of need comes before you.

Bedside Manner in Prayer

It is wise to seek permission before you touch a person in prayer. For some people, touching is perceived as an invasion of privacy. If you want to touch for anointing purposes, just tell the person what you are about to do. When touching a person, only touch the forehead lightly.

Do not press hard with your whole hand on someone's head. Never put pressure on the head to move it backward. Use extreme caution, since the person's neck may have some physical damage already. You don't want to hurt someone by being too aggressive in the laying on of hands! Never push anyone so that they fall. If people should happen to fall under the power of the Holy Spirit, help them to be comfortable, and cover their midsection with a cloth or a jacket. Never, ever try to make falling happen. You are not the Holy Spirit. You are merely a conduit of His power.

Also be very careful about kneeling when you pray for anyone. Kneeling might complicate things, as you may be facing a serious spiritual condition involving evil with this individual, and kneeling signifies submission. We never want to kneel before evil. You can kneel and pray to God before you engage in the ministry of prayer, but be wise about this when praying specifically for someone. The nature of spiritual bondage or the presence of an evil spirit needs to be understood and handled properly. Jesus never knelt before a demon; the demons had to bow before Him. Put very plainly, if you suspect there is demonic involvement, never kneel!

When someone is crying, if tears fall and keep falling, indicating release of deep suffering and contrition, remain close and follow your prayer all the way to the end. The person may desire an embrace. This is perfectly biblical and ethical. You are the hands and arms of a loving Heavenly Father to someone at that moment. Remember, ethics is being aware of who is receiving prayer and how to treat them with respect.

The Art of Waiting

While there is an urgency in the heart of God to reach the lowest and the most desperate, in these latter years of my life, I am realizing that the more I slow down and take my time, the more accurate I become in prayer. Waiting in prayer means that you wait on the Holy Spirit of God. At times we who love to pray for others are in a hurry to hear from God. However, if you follow the ministry of Jesus Christ, you will find that He was never in a hurry.

There are those evenings of ministering in churches when the prayer line seems to stretch around the block! You can tell that you are going to be there for hours. The temptation is to speed through the process so that you can pray for as many people as possible. This is a mistake. The size of the congregation should not dictate the time spent in prayer for them.

Also, waiting on God will bring correction of intent. Pride can easily set in when you see a long line of people wanting prayer and you think they are coming to you, as though you are special and you hold the answer to their healing. If you feel that way, slow down and wait on God. Pride comes before the fall. When you get ahead of the Holy Spirit, pride enters in. The worst experience you can have at the altar is the lack of revelation. When God is moving, you are following. When God is moving, you are hearing. When God is moving, you are accurate. God must receive all of the glory for a healed or transformed life.

At the Altar

The altar area of the church is spiritually charged. It is at this holy place where two lives are joined in marriage, where sinners receive Christ, where saints are baptized, and even where a life is celebrated before the body is taken to the cemetery. It is reflective of the Holy of Holies in Solomon's temple. The presence of God resides in His sanctuary, especially in this altar area.

As I prepare myself for prayer at the altar, I try to scan the faces of those who are coming forward. I am looking for desperation, emptiness, and void. After finding the one the Lord seems to be pointing me to, then I begin to pray. This has been helpful since I trust that if I begin right, I will finish right.

In some services where there are other prayer team members ministering to the people who have come forward, I am aware that the worst need might not be at the altar, but way in the back, on the last pew of the church. In these instances, I leave the altar area, walk to the back of the church, and go directly to the person. I honestly don't think that I have ever been rejected in this approach. They usually are willing to come with me to the front of the church, and we begin to pray there. Accurate prayer involves boldness. Sometimes we must exercise that boldness before the specific revelation comes.

If you are serving as a member of a prayer team, your task is to see where you are needed most. There are always some people in the congregation who want privacy and prefer to pray quietly in their seat, but hopefully the majority respond to the invitation to come forward for prayer. As they come, you can simply ask the question, "Do you want me to pray for you?" As you receive a positive response, first ask the person to raise their face upward. Many people who feel burdened and heavy-laden will stare down at the carpet. But this is their moment to receive something from the Lord, and you want them to assume a posture of receptivity and faith. Help the person to take this posture before the Lord. Also, if they are able, lift both of their hands up. Be aware that certain individuals cannot move their arms up due to a shoulder or arm injury. That is fine, but if they can at least raise their hands a little, take both of their hands into yours and hold them in an open, receptive position. Why is this critical? The person may feel defeated, oppressed, or condemned, and they need to make a break with the passive, morbid attitude, which is reflected in the body. Gently forcing the person to come up out of that introspective physical position can be the launchpad for a great work of the Holy Spirit in that person's life.

Not all problems can be dealt with at the altar. There are circumstances when, if you are going to minister accurately and effectively to someone, privacy is required. A person going through a debilitating trauma is not likely to respond to you if many others can hear what is being said. Every time you have a meeting, a service, or an event in your church or city, set apart a room on the side for more confidential prayer ministry to take place. There should be those on the prayer team who are watching for the most difficult cases, and who can take someone aside when they see that special attention is required.

Ushers at the Altar

These are days in which sorrow and suffering are very present in our churches. Society is changing rapidly. In the past, ushers in the local church were trained to seat newcomers, pass the offering plate, watch the main door, and turn the lights on and off. In the new order of things, many churches are offering training for the ushers on how to be sensitive to the needs of others. When a person is in deep grief, during the sermon or the time of prayer, the usher is trained to approach the individual and make an invitation for him or her to receive prayer. In many of churches that I visit, the ushers are busy praying for those in need even before the service starts.

Ushers should be tuned in to illness that is visible, difficulties in families, and obvious emotional distress that calls for some attention and help. If Walmart can have a greeter at the front door, why not the church of the Lord Jesus Christ? A Walmart greeter can answer your questions and tell you where to find things in the store. Do we expect our ushers in church to be aware of the burdens of others and be active, or are they just flies on the wall in view of a suffering membership?

We speak of serving others, but we cannot think of prayer for others as if prayer was an intrusion into their space. Jesus Christ never asked permission to minister to someone. As society changes, we must change and become more aggressive about offering ministry to anyone with whom we come in contact.

In Brazil, I was about to start praying for several hundred people when I observed a woman approximately forty years of age, bent over with her head to the floor and crying heavily. As I approached her, I asked another woman, who was a leader in the church, to assist me. One look at the woman on the floor and I knew she had been deeply hurt and abused by someone. Discernment of spirits at times such as this operates very fast. In a matter of seconds, I asked her a question, "What is his name?" She let out a loud cry and I brought the other woman close to hold her and embrace her. The situation was being dealt with already. The Holy Spirit is much faster than you think. He was already ministering to her with precision and power. The name of the man did not come out of her mouth, but a great deal of pain did come out.

When the assisting woman tried to help her up off the floor, she screamed, as though she was being hurt. The Holy Spirit communicated to me that her husband had physically abused her. Do not ask me how this could come so easily. All I know is that God was in a hurry to help this woman. I asked the assisting woman to take her to another room and inspect her condition more carefully. She returned to tell me that the woman's body was full of bruises. My job now was to bring healing to her and her husband.

As it turns out, the husband was one of the ushers standing at the back of the church. I went to him and brought him to the room where his wife was resting in a chair. I called for the pastor, which is always the thing to do in these kinds of serious cases, so that he will be in the loop and be involved. Together we began to pray for this couple. After a while the pastor took the husband to another room, and I proceeded with my prayer for the wife. More tears and more pain came from her.

The couple eventually had to be separated for a time, but they were reunited months later. He submitted to the pastor and received the right counseling for his problems, and the woman was also cared for in prayer.

Anyone who opens the door for the Holy Spirit to work will have similar experiences in ministry. The local pastor who knows the congregation can minister to them and be much more effective than an itinerant evangelist. When conviction sets in, people are changed by the very presence of God. However, we can play an important part by honoring God's people with simple principles of wisdom, gentleness, and good ethics. Results come from working with people, loving people, and following the leading of the Holy Spirit.

16

The Principle of Authority

Power and Authority

Authority is the accurate implementation of power in ministry. When you see a large rocket about to take off from Cape Canaveral in Florida, you are seeing power being directed accurately. Without the instruments to guide the rocket into its proper orbit, all you have is power with no direction. In ministry, authority is guided power. This concept of power and authority must be clearly understood in order to bring about accuracy in personal prayer ministry.

When the apostle Paul said, "For I am not ashamed of the gospel, for it is the power of God for salvation to everyone who believes, to the Jew first and also to the Greek" (Rom. 1:16), he was saying that the power of God is a mighty force that directs its strength to meet the needs of people and accomplish the will of God. Note Paul's language: "power of God for salvation." The greatest miracle is when someone is changed by the power of God—no longer living lost. Now, there is real life in Christ.

Guided Power

Raw power is common. A locomotive has raw power. It pulls hundreds of cars behind it. It can slow down or it can speed up, but it has to stay within the rails. Out of the rail, the locomotive will not move anywhere. Guided power has no rails. You cannot contain it, you cannot make it do anything, you cannot tell it to go faster or slower. It is power with the ability to remember, act, and retract in order to accomplish the task at hand. This power knows all.

The only way to connect to it is to be able to follow its path and simply obey its commands. Whatever it does, you do the same. You cannot create a path. The path is created by the power itself. This power is the Holy Spirit. You can partake of it, but it does not mean you own it or control it. It controls you. That is the concept of guided power.

It is the desire of the heart of God to do His work with your help. He calls and appoints you and me as His ministers, that we might administrate His Word and His power. But in no way is that power under our control. When God wants to save, He will save without you. When He heals, He will heal without you. If that is the case, why does God require our participation? Very simply, He wants us to work in fellowship with Him to fulfill His will in the lives of others. That is why the Lord Jesus dealt with the concept of servanthood so much. It is in serving that we please the heart of God. We are called to serve God—whatever He needs, whatever He wants, anytime, any day, anywhere.

He is in control; we are not. Do you really want to experience praying with accuracy? If you do, then please set your mind upon this concept right away. If there is an area of spiritual endeavor that you cannot control, it is the work of the Holy Spirit. Your goal must not be to possess power, but to be a servant.

The questions I am asked the most about guided power are as follows: What is required in order for me to partake of this guided power concept? Does it work for everyone, or is it only for a select few? How does guided power actually work? Of course, there are many other questions, but these are a few for us to consider.

What Is Required to Partake of the Ministry of the Holy Spirit?

The most required ingredient you will need in order to partake of guided power is respect. Ignoring this ingredient has closed more doors to prayer seekers than any other. You do not have to understand guided power, but you must respect it. In the hills of Virginia lives a Methodist preacher and personal friend, a man named Buster Payne. Buster worked for many years as a lineman for the power company. This meant daily contact with power wires, repairing the electric grid of Virginia by climbing one hundred feet in the air, working closely with thousands of watts of power. He told me once that he could take a spoon and extend it close to the wire and the spoon would melt before his very eyes. Just like those hot wires, guided power has to be respected. You have to be very careful and very aware of what it can do.

The Holy Spirit is more powerful than all of the electrical grids in the world, and yet He is the most persecuted part of the Trinity. In so many places, the Holy Spirit is not taught about, invited, or allowed to manifest His presence in our churches, as if He is a plague to be avoided. Those who act in this way toward the Holy Spirit become blind and ineffectual. God in His mercy can still use them, but on a very small scale. Having an attitude of no respect for the power of God found in the Holy Spirit will lead you nowhere in praying with accuracy.

Andrew Murray wrote, "The Church has lost the note of authority, the secret of wisdom, and the gift of power through its persistent and willful neglect of the Holy Spirit of God."[1]

Does It Work for Everyone, or Just a Select Few?

It is amazing that the most simple-minded person can participate in the presence of God, and yet those who are well-educated frequently have problems with the Holy Spirit. For many years of my life I fell into that category. I was well-educated, with several master's degrees, but I resisted hearing about or considering the nature and work of the Holy Spirit. What made me skeptical was pressure from my peers in the American church. It seemed that the status quo would not allow any free expression in worship, prayer, or even preaching. Yet as a young man from Brazil, accustomed to rhythm and dancing in the church, it all was very confusing to me.

Anyone with a willing and humble heart will hear from God, but the proud will be denied. Hearing comes when you are quiet and still in your soul. The sometimes counterproductive activity of liturgy, repetitive procedures, and programs can levy a deadly effect upon hearing God. A total lack of freedom in worship causes the churchgoer to think that God must be very formal, austere, and dry, with no creativity. It makes one think that there is a pipe organ playing a solemn dirge in heaven and that God only likes that pipe organ.

In the area of Sitio Grande, Cuba, resides a Methodist pastor in his early fifties. His name is Javier Canibe. For six years, he has led a house church as part of the hundreds of house churches forming within the Cuban Methodist Church. Javier is humble and unassuming. He lives in a house made of cardboard. This man is full of the presence of God. Hundreds have come to know Jesus through his small ministry. The political scene in Cuba may be oppressive, but within the church the Holy Spirit is free to move and the result is a great harvest of souls.

How Is Guided Power Implemented?

I am so glad that I do not have to bring people into the moment of catharsis. God does that so much better than I. The most wonderful benefit of guided power prayer is that I can pray with accuracy for the worst need and do not have to deal for hours or days or months with all of the ramifications of the matter. God does that. He does the complete healing in the life of a person.

Philippians 2:13 says, "For it is God who is at work in you, both to will and to work for His good pleasure." To have to investigate, analyze, and discuss all of the consequences of problems within an individual or family will consume time and will psychologically deplete your energies. When your mind is trying to solve a problem for someone instead of asking the Holy Spirit to show you the real need, you are missing your target. The Holy Spirit does accurate, detailed work, and He does it much better than the best of us. There is no human mind that can do better than the Spirit of God.

You may remember a story I shared with you in chapter 6 about the root of unforgiveness. Allow me to repeat this story, this time with a different emphasis. In Van Buren, Arkansas, I was doing counseling at the pastor's office. A lady came in and asked me to pray for her. She said a few words, but the sound of her voice is what caught my attention.

She also grasped her hands tightly and looked at me with anxiety in her face. I asked about her family and she began to tell me about them. I did not really have to hear the words because the tension and stress in her voice told me everything. I had to begin with her most immediate pain. I discerned that her need was relational. In that moment, I heard from the Lord, "She has not talked with her sister for many years."

The root here was unforgiveness, so I told her that it was imperative for her to go to her sister's house, ask forgiveness, and bring an end to the disagreement between them. She began to cry. This had to be from the Lord. No one could have known or even come close to discovering this family secret. They had kept the family feud hidden for the sake of a good image. She went directly to her sister and God healed their relationship that day. She later wrote a detailed testimony about her experience, which was published in the bulletin of the church. I could have talked with her about her concerns for her son, conflict with her husband over finances, and many other details and goings-on within the family, but God wanted unforgiveness out of the way first! The fruits of that prayer produced healing in the whole family.

That time of prayer took about fifteen minutes. Was it effective? Yes, very effective! God was in that room to help me. Did I hear from Him? Oh yes, I did, and I heard accurately. Did He do great work? In fact, He did ninety-nine percent of the work in the family completely without me. I am a one-percent Christian, and happy to be one!

When you have identified the proper root, guided power takes over. Since I knew it was unforgiveness, now I simply had to wait for direction. Guided power automatically connects you to the need. The focus of unforgiveness is not toward an object or a thing. It has to be toward a person. Begin with family, since unforgiveness between siblings is very offensive to the Holy Spirit.

Authority Is What Jesus Does

What kind of power do you use when you pray? Maybe you repeat words that throughout the years have become your way of communicating a prayer. Perhaps you utilize techniques that you know will influence and cause certain responses from others, or you bring a person through regression—calling up, reliving, and remembering trauma from years ago.

However, under guided power, there is much less of you and much more of God. The Holy Spirit is the Spirit of Jesus. The power we are talking about refers to the all of the words, miracles, and parables of Jesus. It encompasses His existence with God from eternity past, His virgin conception and birth, sinless life, perfect ministry, atoning death, resurrection from the dead, ascension to glory, and His promise to come again to rule over all of creation. All of these put together make up the power that resides in Jesus Christ alone. In ministry, power is authority—but it is not your authority. We have an erroneous concept that ministering in authority is something that we do. Under guided power, authority is what Jesus does. It is completely different from manmade power, and the results will surprise you. Under guided power, God does more and you do less.

Ministering the gospel is exercising the authority given to us as ambassadors of Christ. "Therefore, we are ambassadors for Christ, as though God were making an appeal through us; we beg you on behalf of Christ, be reconciled to God" (2 Cor. 5:20a). An ambassador has the authority to speak for the one whom he or she represents. For example, the United States' ambassador to Japan has the authority to speak for the president of the United States. It is understood that he or she will speak according to the will and policy of the president. Likewise, exercising authority in the name of Jesus means that we operate in the will of God, representing His intention and His loving character. The authority given to believers is similar to a power of attorney, which is given by one person to another so that the latter can act on behalf of the former. In this regard, Jesus has given us power to act on His behalf for the sake of others. "Jesus summoned His twelve disciples and gave them authority over unclean spirits, to cast them out, and to heal every kind of disease and every kind of sickness" (Matt. 10:1).

As you arrive at a greater understanding of the authority given through the name of Jesus, the power in your ministry will increase.

Discovering that demons and every disease are subject to the name of Jesus gives new boldness and confidence in prayer and ministry. This confidence is not in any man but in God. In Matthew 10:1, "Jesus summoned His twelve disciples and gave them authority." Jesus gave His disciples the power of attorney to act on His behalf. This does not mean that we are to take over, but instead, we are to represent Him. To represent Him, you must follow His commands and wishes in the prayer that you speak over someone else. It does not say you are going to heal, but that you are going to represent Christ. He is the one who heals.

I cannot emphasize enough that power is authority recognized only in the person of Jesus. All that we do in ministry is directly related to the power found in Jesus Christ. The power does not come from us; only the implementation of it has been given to us. We are the extension of Jesus' ministry. We are His voice to say what He wants to say and His hands and feet to do what He wants to do. He conducts ministry in us, for us, and through us. The meaning of John 14:12 becomes clear when interpreted this way: "Truly, truly, I say to you, he who believes in Me, the works that I do, he will do also; and greater works than these he will do; because I go to the Father."

I met a pastor who preached in a certain church for a period of four years. The members loved him and were saddened to find out he was going to move somewhere else. Upon his departure, the congregation began to leave the church. Within a period of eighteen months, the attendees decreased from eight hundred members to one hundred and fifty members. Why did this take place? If you had ever heard him preach, you would understand. His preaching was spellbinding and captivating, centered upon him and his entertaining stories. His personality was larger than life and stronger than any presence of God in the room. The people fell in love with him but they did not know Jesus. They were engaged in listening to this skilled preacher, but they did not know who Christ was, what He could do for them, and that it was He who deserved their devotion. This is a good example of how much you must disappear so that God can do His ministry through you. Under guided power, you are not promoting yourself or pleasing anyone. You are being the hands and feet of the Savior. He is to receive all of the glory.

Authority and Heaven

> And Jesus came up and spoke to them, saying, "All authority has been given to Me in heaven and on earth. Go therefore and make disciples of all the nations, baptizing them in the name of the Father and the Son and the Holy Spirit, teaching them to observe all that I commanded you; and lo, I am with you always, even to the end of the age." (Matt. 28:18–20)

The authority given to His followers by Jesus involves heavenly and earthly authority. In Jesus Christ, all levels of authority reside. Notice also that the text puts authority in the context of accomplishing ministry. "Go therefore and make disciples" refers to a command that can only be put into action because of the fact that all authority is found in Jesus Christ. The power available to you to make disciples rests upon your understanding of Jesus Christ—who He was in His earthly ministry being led by the Holy Spirit, and who He is now as He sits at the right hand of the Father (see Hebrews 1:3).

Since authority is based on the person of Jesus Christ and His power, grasping the meaning of Matthew 16:13–19 is essential:

> Now when Jesus came into the district of Caesarea Philippi, He was asking His disciples, "Who do people say that the Son of Man is?" And they said, "Some say John the Baptist; and others, Elijah; but still others, Jeremiah, or one of the

prophets." He said to them, "But who do you say that I am?" Simon Peter answered, "You are the Christ, the Son of the living God." And Jesus said to him, "Blessed are you, Simon Barjona, because flesh and blood did not reveal this to you, but My Father who is in heaven. I also say to you that you are Peter, and upon this rock I will build My church; and the gates of Hades will not overpower it. I will give you the keys of the kingdom of heaven; and whatever you shall bind on earth shall be bound in heaven, and whatever you shall loose on earth shall be loosed in heaven."

First, this scripture indicates that knowing the person of Jesus Christ comes only by revelation from God. After two-and-one-half years of hearing Jesus preach, seeing Him work miracles, and then witnessing the transfiguration, Peter finally believed. One day, as he stood in the region of Caesarea Philippi, Jesus Christ was made known to him. Only upon this basis, Jesus tells Peter, has he now become a candidate for authority. Thus, any hope of exercising true authority first depends upon a revelation of Jesus Christ coming into your life.

Second, Jesus speaks to Peter about building His church through revelation, not manmade concepts. Therefore, when you exercise authority on the basis of your revelation of who Jesus is, what you do is not of yourself, nor of any human institution. It comes directly to you from God. Many people can teach you, set an example to imitate, and help to prepare you. But, in the end, the only way you will be able to operate in true authority is by a revelation of Jesus Christ to you personally—which comes from Him alone.

After this revelation is given, Jesus then says He will "give you the keys of the kingdom of heaven" (v. 19). Why a key? What does a key do? A key gives access. If there is a locked door, the key gives access to whatever lies behind that door. In this case, the key offered by Jesus gives the believer access to the entire kingdom of heaven! When you pray, you are accessing heaven for the purpose of ministry. If this concept of authority is to be of any use, it has to be through our ability to gain access and connect with God in prayer through Jesus Christ.

Jesus goes on to say that this type of prayer refers to whatever you choose to bind or loose. The Greek word translated "to bind" is the same root word for "supplication," "intercession," or "petition" (as in Ephesians 6:18: "With all prayer and petition pray at all times in the Spirit, and with this in view, be on the alert with all perseverance and petition for all the saints"). Therefore, according to Matthew 16:19, whatever you petition, intercede for, or bind on earth (when it is based upon revelation from God), will be spoken in the same manner in heaven. This seems to be too grand to accept but, in reality, it is the key to your prayer of faith. You speak the word given by revelation and the same word is repeated in heaven. Authority, then, begins and ends in heaven and is implemented in prayer. That is why I use the term "guided power." You are not guiding—God is.

Likewise, Jesus says, "Whatever you shall loose on earth shall be loosed in heaven" (v. 19). The Greek word translated "loose" is also translated "destroy" in 1 John 3:8b: "The Son of God appeared for this purpose, to destroy the works of the devil."

The prayer of authority based upon revelation of Jesus Christ is the key to accessing heaven in order to loose (or set free) the one in bondage, and to bind (or supplicate, intercede, petition) God's purpose and will to be done for the individual in Jesus' name.

Revelation by the Holy Spirit

The concept of authority cannot be separated from revelation, which comes by the Holy Spirit. Imagine that you are trying to make a reservation to fly to somewhere in Europe based upon the idea that there might be a flight sometime during the day that could take you there.

Here you have a general idea of the means of travel and the direction you want to go, but these facts alone are not enough for you to make a reservation. In order to make a reservation, you will have to know the exact destination, the dates and times of departure and return, and the name and contact information for the airline with which you want your reservation to be made.

This same analogy holds true regarding the implementation of authority to meet a need. It is difficult to begin a prayer without adequate information about the person receiving the prayer, or the destination of that prayer.

The connection between revelation and authority may seem rather obscure and foreign to many since we often only pray based upon our feelings and emotions. To someone who prays out of his or her feelings, revelation will be a compelling discovery. Authority is based upon revelation, and revelation depends upon intimacy or connectivity with God through Jesus Christ. Because revelation is the work of the Holy Spirit, we can only experience it when we accept the third person of the Trinity, the Holy Spirit, as essential to any act of ministry or prayer. Observe that I am referring to the Holy Spirit of God and not "the spirit," as though it could be any spiritual entity. I have deep respect for the third person of the Trinity. There are many ways that revelation comes to a human being, including dreams, visions, angels, the inner voice, a prophetic voice, and Scripture. But in all forms of revelation from God the Father, it is through Jesus Christ the Son, imparted to the believer by the Holy Spirit, consistent with the Word of God.

Revelation is given to the person who is praying for someone, in order to help him or her meet the need at hand. Revelation is the act of the Holy Spirit initializing, directing, and completing your prayer. The Holy Spirit is eager to communicate! He is eager to share direction and purpose in prayer, and He is eager to complete the prayer, because He is in the business of healing and restoring people.

The gifts of the Holy Spirit—especially those of revelation—will operate in any act of ministry where the name of Jesus Christ is honored and revered.

Revelation comes by faith. You must believe that you are able to receive revelation from God. It is not so much that you hear a voice, but more often a thought or concept comes into your mind. Much of it comes through an active knowledge of the Word of God, because one of the most common ways in which the Holy Spirit speaks is through Scripture. He will bring a Scripture to mind that gives amazingly clear direction to you as you begin to pray. Sometimes a single word mentioned to the person receiving prayer will cause a strong emotional response. This confirms the revelation, letting you know that you are on the right track.

In short, here are three principles of revelation, merged with authority in ministry: 1) revelation from God pertaining to ministry is accurate and specific, and unique to the case at hand. When the believer exercises authority with precision and accuracy, based upon revelation, the ministry will bring conviction and will bear witness to the one who receives the prayer; 2) revelation is not given for its own sake. It is given in order to benefit the life of someone else. To desire revelation for its own sake without exercising authority is a self-serving ministry, without love for people. It is sterile and will not minister to anyone or produce fruit. On the other hand, you can be confident that if God reveals and you respond sincerely by exercising authority for the benefit of others, you will see positive results most of the time; and 3) revelation and authority depend upon each other. Revelation from God communicates the urgency of the moment, gives specific direction and procedure, and conveys information about completing the prayer. The gifts of the Holy Spirit are tools to inform the person praying so that the power of God can be correctly discharged through authority. Supernatural knowledge given through revelation has a definite purpose: the completion of the prayer in authority. This pattern of revelation leading to command and authority is seen consistently in the ministry of Jesus.

The apostle Paul, in conveying this concept of the place of revelation in his own ministry, writes in Romans 1:16–17, "For I am not ashamed of the gospel, for it is the power of God for salvation to everyone who believes, to the Jew first and also to the Greek. For in it the righteousness of God is revealed from faith to faith; as it is written, 'But the righteous man shall live by faith.'" Effective ministry that meets the deepest needs of others is by faith. It is by faith that one receives the necessary revelation from the Holy Spirit and then moves to complete the act of ministry with authority. It is by this faith that the "power of God unto salvation" is transmitted into the lives of individuals for whom we pray, so as to see them restored to wholeness.

I met a young man who had much pride and hardness within him. The pride was something he had developed in order to compensate for his father's departure from his life when he was seven years of age. His hardness of heart became evident as he repeatedly resisted any spiritual authority from any man or woman of God. Because this area in his life had never been dealt with, he refused to acknowledge his superiors, even pastors who wished to bless him and help him. He had his own ideas, and though he claimed to hear directly from God, his hearing was not accurate because he resisted the Holy Spirit in his mind. No efforts to convince him of this reality have been successful. His life will be deeply affected by his rebellion until he is willing to receive what the Holy Spirit has revealed regarding his deepest need.

If you question or resist that it is the Holy Spirit who makes manifest the relationship with God the Father through His Son Jesus Christ, you will never walk in the authority intended for all believers by our Lord. Further, you will be unable to benefit from and respond to those who have been placed in authority by God to bring healing and empowerment to you. Recognizing the chain of command that begins in heaven and ends with a servant who is submitted to the Holy Spirit is key.

His Responsibility—Our Response

Crucial to our understanding of authority is the reality that when God gives accurate discernment regarding a need, it is His responsibility to meet that need. The purest definition of authority is this: if you are under authority, someone else is above you. If you have a need that must be met, the person in rank above you has the sole responsibility to solve your dilemma. All you have to do is to go to the person above you and relay the problem. The one in authority is responsible for the well-being of those who look to him in trust and obedience. This is supposed to be true in military ranks, and it is true in the order of the kingdom of God. Authority in this sense is always the heart of God. The proper place of authority is not to lord it over, but to meet the need.

The application of authority means issuing a command under the authority given to us by Jesus Christ. Exercising authority means that one speaks specific words into a situation that affirm the authority of Christ. However, contrary to what you might think, a command is a response rather than a statement. This is because it does not begin with you. It already began in heaven. In other words, you are responding to and applying what you have understood, experienced, and come to believe regarding the ministry, life, death, and resurrection of Jesus Christ. When discernment has taken place, the Holy Spirit shows you His will and what to say in each particular situation, providing direction for the prayer or act of ministry.

Richard J. Foster wrote, "In Authoritative Prayer we are calling forth the will of the Father upon the earth. Here we are not so much speaking *to* God as speaking *for* God. We are not asking God to do something; rather, we are using the authority of God to command something done."[2]

Exercising Authority

A command comes out of your personal conviction that Jesus is who He says He is. In Acts 3:6–8, the apostle Peter, speaking to the lame man at the gate called Beautiful, declares:

> "I do not possess silver and gold, but what I do have I give to you: In the name of Jesus Christ the Nazarene—walk!" And seizing him by the right hand, he raised him up; and immediately his feet and his ankles were strengthened. With a leap he stood upright and began to walk; and he entered the temple with them, walking and leaping and praising God.

As the apostle Peter looked upon a suffering man, he said to himself, "What I do have to give?" What was it that Peter had? Peter did not have money. But Peter had personal, intimate experience with Jesus of Nazareth—His ministry, death, burial, resurrection, and ascension. By personal revelation, he had a solid, unwavering knowledge of Jesus in His fullness. Peter also had received the infusion of power given by the Holy Spirit at Pentecost.

Because of all this, upon seeing the predicament of the lame man, Peter responded not to the man's request for alms, but to who he knew Jesus Christ to be. Peter understood that he possessed not what the man was asking for, but what the man needed. The man was only hoping to subsist for one more day by receiving a handout. But God wanted the man completely restored to wholeness. God always wants to do more than we even think or imagine! A revelation from heaven enabled Peter to speak to the man's true need with authority.

This demonstrates why authority is directly connected to your interpretation of Scripture and your understanding of it in the light of the Holy Spirit. The success of any prayer ministry is dependent upon exercising authority in the name of Jesus. Authority releases the power, but always remember that it is not the power of the one praying. It is the power found only in the person of the crucified and resurrected Son of God.

This pattern of authority implemented through command is observed repeatedly in the ministry of Jesus. Seventy-five percent of the miracles and healings performed by Jesus occurred when He pronounced a command of authority.

> When the woman saw that she had not escaped notice, she came trembling and fell down before Him, and declared in the presence of all the people the reason why she had touched Him, and how she had been immediately healed. And He said to her, "Daughter, your faith has made you well; go in peace." (Luke 8:47–48)

Jesus gives this woman perhaps the greatest gift of all for a person with a root of rejection: peace. The meaning of the Hebrew word *shalom* encompasses peace, completeness, prosperity, welfare, tranquility, and wholeness. Therefore, the command given to this woman by Jesus is to go and walk in wholeness. A woman who had suffered for so long and had spent all of her money, only to be ostracized by her community for at least twelve years, has just been told by the Master that she is somebody! With this simple command, Jesus looses the woman from her infirmity and releases healing to her emotions and wholeness into her life.

"When Jesus saw that a crowd was rapidly gathering, He rebuked the unclean spirit, saying to it, 'You deaf and mute spirit, I command you, come out of him and do not enter him again'" (Mark 9:25).

Command and authority is seen as Jesus commands the evil spirit to come out of the demon-possessed boy and never return to him. The response to Jesus' command and the evidence of His authority is seen in the next verse when the evil spirit comes out with a cry.

A biblical understanding of authority is badly needed within the body of Christ today. Liberal theology has taught us to only be tolerant and compassionate toward someone in bondage and overlooks the authority given to the believer to set the prisoner free and to destroy the works of the devil in his or her life. Authority means that we are not to just comfort those trapped in sin and sadness, but that we possess within ourselves the fullness of Jesus Christ, who came to heal the brokenhearted and to declare liberty to the captive. Authority is a bridge that transmits the raw power of God to the one in need.

When you grasp this biblical principle of authority, you will find that you are liberated—freed from the intimidating and frustrating effort to try to generate results in ministry in and of yourself. When you know that you know, beyond any doubt, that all authority belongs to Jesus, and not to you, faith suddenly rises! You will begin a new adventure of exercising this principle in faith when ministering to someone. It is not a doctrine; it is who you are in the act of conducting ministry— you are connected to almighty God in heaven through Jesus Christ. You can be several things when ministering to someone, but you cannot be doubtful regarding the person of Jesus. Your application of authority relies upon who Jesus Christ is, was, and will be in your life.

In closing, I want to encourage you by assuring you that your prayer, counseling, and ministry will radically change when authority is established and put into practice. I know that you want to see people's lives genuinely transformed by the power of the Word and the Holy Spirit. As you conduct any act of ministry, the knowledge that you are responding to revelation from heaven and transmitting the authority given to you in the person of Jesus Christ will produce ministry that is efficient, accurate, and powerful.

We have covered many essential principles in this book: spiritual and relational needs; the four roots of rejection, rebellion, unforgiveness, and bitterness, a methodology of ministry repeated over and over by our Lord; how to minister to the soul; ethics of prayer; and how to break through in prayer by exercising your authority as a believer.

Are you ready to begin implementing these biblical principles in your own ministry? Can you dare to believe that God will use you to minister to the deepest needs of people the same way Jesus did, by the power of the same Holy Spirit? I did not learn all of this in one day and neither will you. However, I have full confidence that if you are willing to be an obedient and humble instrument in the hand of God, He will amaze you. As you honor Him and the biblical principles set forth in this book, He will honor you and give you fruit.

May God bless you, and may He receive all of the glory!

BIBLIOGRAPHY

Abraham, William J. *Wesley for Armchair Theologians.* Louisville, KY: Westminster: John Knox Press, 2005.

Bounds, Edward McKendree. *The Complete Works of E. M. Bounds on Prayer.* Grand Rapids, MI: Baker Books, 2004.

Chadwick, Samuel. *The Way to Pentecost.* Fort Washington, PA: CLC Publications, 2001.

Cowman, L. B. *Streams in the Desert.* Edited by James Riemann. Grand Rapids, MI: Zondervan, 1997.

Foster, Richard J. *Prayer—Finding the Heart's True Home.* San Francisco, CA: HarperCollins, 1992.

Hedland, Leif. *Healing the Orphan Spirit.* Peachtree City, GA: Global Mission Awareness, 2013.

Law, William. *The Power of the Holy Spirit.* Edited by Dave Hunt. Fort Washington, PA: CLC Publications, 2006.

Manser, Martin H., ed. *The Westminster Collection of Christian Quotations.* Louisville, KY: Westminster John Knox Press, 2001.

Moody, Dwight Lyman. *Secret Power.* New Kensington, PA: Whitaker House, 1997.

Murray, Andrew. *Absolute Surrender.* Minneapolis, MI: Bethany House, 2003.

———. *Humility.* New Kensington, PA: Whitaker House, 1982.

———. *Reaching Your World for Christ.* New Kensington, PA: Whitaker House, 1997.

———. *The Spirit of Christ.* Kensington, PA: Whitaker House, 1984.

———. *With Christ in the School of Prayer.* New Kensington, PA: Whitaker House, 1981.

Strong, Douglas M. et al. *Reclaiming the Wesleyan Tradition: John Wesley's Sermons for Today.* Nashville, TN: Discipleship Resources, 2007.

Torrey, R. A. *How to Pray.* Accessed August 21, 2015. www.ccel. org/ccel/torrey/pray.html.

———. *The Presence and Work of the Holy Spirit.* Kensington, PA: Whitaker House, 1996.

Turnbull, Ralph, ed. *The Best of D. L.* Moody. Grand Rapids, MI: Baker Books, 1971.

Zuck, Roy B. *The Speaker's Quote Book: Over 5,000 Illustrations for All Occasions.* Grand Rapids, MI: Kregel Publications, 1997.

Notes

Chapter One

1. F. B. Meyer in Roy B. Zuck's, *The Speaker's Quote Book: Over 4,500 Illustrations and Quotations for All Occasions* (Grand Rapids, MI: Kregel Publications, 1997), 222.
2. Andrew Murray, quoted in L. B. Cowman, *Streams in the Desert*, ed. James Reimann (1925; repr., Grand Rapids, MI: Zondervan, 1996), 413.
3. Samuel Chadwick, *The Way to Pentecost* (1932; repr., Fort Washington, PA: CLC Publications, 2001), 28.
4. Extra Sensory Perception: "perception or communication outside of normal sensory capability, as in telepathy and clairvoyance."
5. R. A. Torrey, "How to Pray," Chapter II. Christian Classics Ethereal Library, accessed August 21, 2015, www.ccel.org/ccel/torrey/pray.html.
6. William Law, *The Power of the Spirit*, ed. Dave Hunt (Fort Washington, PA: CLC Publications, 2006), 24. William Law wrote that "a failure to realize that our salvation can only be worked out by the power of the indwelling Holy Spirit forming the very life of Christ within the redeemed heart has placed the Christian church in the same apostasy that characterized the Jewish nation."
7. Andrew Murray, *Absolute Surrender* (repr., Grand Rapids, MI: Bethany House Publishers, 2003), 13.

Chapter Two

1. John Wesley, "The Almost Christian" (1741), Preached at St. Mary's, Oxford, on July 25, 1741, in Douglas M. Strong et al, *Reclaiming the Wesleyan Tradition: John Wesley's Sermons for Today* (Nashville, TN: Discipleship Resources, 2007) 56–59.
2. Leif Hetland, *Healing the Orphan Spirit: The Father Wants His Kids Back* (Peachtree City, GA: Global Mission Awareness, 2013), 23–24.

Chapter Three

1. Andrew Murray, *Reaching Your World for Christ* (reprint, New Kensington, PA: Whitaker House, 1997), 107.

Chapter Six

1. Andrew Murray, *With Christ in the School of Prayer* (reprint, New Kensington, PA: Whitaker House, 1981), 107.

Chapter Eight

1. George Müller in Roy B. Zuck, *The Speaker's Quote Book: Over 5,000 Illustrations and Quotations for All Occasions* (Grand Rapids, MI: Kregel Publications, 1997), 185.
2. William J. Abraham, *Wesley for Armchair Theologians* (Louisville, KY: Westminster John Knox Press, 2005), 51. Abraham wrote, "God has moved in 'prevenient' grace, in the grace that comes before the actual deep healing made available in Christ through the Holy Spirit, to enable us to see our current predicament and to take the first steps towards our recovery." God moves first toward us to help us begin to move toward Him.
3. Martin H. Manser, ed., *The Westminster Collection of Christian Quotations* (Louisville, KY: Westminster John Knox Press, 2001), 287.
4. R. A. Torry, *The Presence and Work of the Holy Spirit* (reprint, New Kensington, PA: Whitaker House, 1996), 8.

Chapter Nine

1. Andrew Murray, *Humility* (reprint, New Kensington, PA: Whitaker House, 1982), 35.

Chapter Fourteen

1. Ralph Turnbull, ed., *The Best of D. L. Moody* (Grand Rapids, MI: Baker Books, 1971) chapter 8, Witnessing in Power, 89, accessed August 25, 2015, www.ccel.us/moody.ch7.html.

Chapter Fifteen

1. Edward McKendree Bounds, *The Complete Works of E. M. Bounds on Prayer* (Grand Rapids, MI: Baker Books, 1990), 325.
2. Andrew Murray, *Humility* (reprint, New Kensington, PA: Whitaker House, 1982), 44.

Chapter Sixteen

1. Andrew Murray, *Humility* (reprint, New Kensington, PA: Whitaker House, 1982), 44.
2. Richard J. Foster, *Prayer—Finding the Heart's True Home* (San Francisco, CA: HarperCollins, 1992), 229.

About the Author

Ricardo A. "Rick" Bonfim was born in Rio de Janeiro, Brazil, on January 1, 1944. After immigrating to the United States, he received a bachelor of arts degree from Valdosta State College and Florida State University and a masters of divinity degree from Emory University, Atlanta, Georgia. He then received a masters degree in speech communications from the University of Georgia, as well as the ABJ degree in journalism from the University of Georgia.

Rick was ordained an elder in the United Methodist Church in 1980. For thirty-five years he has served full-time as a general evangelist in the North Georgia Conference of the United Methodist Church.

In 2012, Rick received the Phillip Award from the National Association of United Methodists.

Rick Bonfim is the founder and president of Rick Bonfim Ministries, Inc., located in Watkinsville, Georgia. RBM is an international missions agency, which has provided discipleship and life-changing missions opportunities to thousands of people.

CPSIA information can be obtained
at www.ICGtesting.com
Printed in the USA
FSHW021436210619